Californian's
Tale

and other stories

Mark Twain (Florida, Missouri 1835 – Redding, Connecticut 1910), pen-name of Samuel Langhorn Clemens, spent his boyhood by the Mississipi river, which, in those years, was the great high-road of American life. The fascination of the river became one of the central themes in Twain's writing. The term he choose as his pen-name, "mark twain", means "by the mark two fathoms", an expression used by Mississipi riverboat pilots in sounding shallows for minimum navigable depths: it was essentialy a humorous pseudonym.

In his youth he led an adventurous life, travelling and contribuiting to several newspapers.

He had a two-fold personality, he was adventurous and nostalgic, a humourist and a misanthrope, devoted to progress and democracy and a fatalist.

Mark Twain's most important works include: *The Celebrated Jumping Frog of Calaveras County and Other Sketches* (1867); *The Innocence Abroad, or the New Pilgrim's Progress* (1869); *The Adventures of Tom Sawyer* (1876); *Life on the Mississipi* (1883); *The Adventures of Huckleberry Finn* (1884), which is regarded as his masterpiece; *A Connecticut Yankee at King Arthur's Court* (1889); *The Tragedy of Pudd'nhead Wilson* (1889), which is more and more being regarded as one of the major works of fiction of the nineteenth century; *The Man that Corrupted Hadleyburg and Other Stories and Sketches* (1906).

Mark Twain introduced the use of dialect in his works, used new American words and expressed the typical southern American drawl (i. e. a slow way of speech, obtained prolonging the vowel sounds). However his works are not provincial, his characters, although typical of the South, are also universal.

It was once customary to denigrate Mark Twain as a "mere" humourist, but now he is regarded as a towering figure among American novelists.

The importance of Twain's work is well expressed by Hemingway, who said that modern American literature "begins with Huckleberry Finn".

LaSpiga

The Californian's Tale

Thirty-five years ago I was out prospecting on the Stanislaus, tramping all day long with pick and pan and horn, and washing a hatful of dirt here and there, always expecting to make a rich strike, and never doing it. It was a lovely region, woodsy, balmy, delicious, and had once been populous, long years before, but now the people had vanished and the charming paradise was a solitude. They went away when the surface diggings gave out. In one place, where a busy little city with banks and newspapers and fire companies and a mayor and aldermen had been, was nothing but a wide expanse of emerald turf,with not even the faintest sign that human life had ever been present there. This was down toward Tuttletown. In the country neighborhood thereabouts, along the dusty roads, one found at intervals the prettiest little cottage homes, snug and cozy, and so cobwebbed with vines snowed thick with roses that the doors and windows were wholly hidden from sight – sign that these were deserted homes, forsaken years ago by defeated and disappointed families who could neither sell them nor give them away. Now and then, half an hour apart, one came across solitary log cabins of the earliest mining days, built by the first gold-miners, the predecessors of the cottage-builders. In some few cases these cabins were still occupied; and when this was so, you could depend upon it that the occupant was the very pioneer who had built the cabin; and you could depend on another thing,

tale: story.

prospecting: exploring for gold.
Stanislaus: river in North-California. **tramping**: walking. **pick and pan and horn**: equipment used by gold prospectors. **hatful**: quantity contained in a hat. **to make a rich strike**: (informal) to be successful. **woodsy**: with woods. **balmy**: with good air.
populous: inhabited by a lot of people.
vanished: disappeared. **charming**: attractive; enchanting.
diggings: (plural noun) gold mining. **gave out**: was estinguished. **busy**: active.
fire companies: (U.S.) organized bodies of firemen. **mayor**: first citizen. **aldermen**: members of the local council. **turf**: ground.
faintest: weakest; most feeble.
toward: in direction of.
neighborhood: surroundings. **one**: impersonal pronoun.
prettiest: nicest.
snug and cozy: warm and comfortable. **cobwebbed**: covered.
wholly: completely. **hidden from sight**: impossible to be seen.
deserted: abandoned.   **forsaken**: abandoned.
defeated and disappointed: who hadn't met their expectations.
neither...nor: structure used to join together *two negative ideas.*
came across: found by chance. **log cabins**: simple houses constructed out of trunks.
predecessors: those who came before. **In some few cases**: in a small number of cases.
depend upon it: be sure. **the very pioneer**: exactly the pioneer.
cabin: small and poor house. **depend on**: be sure of.

too – that he was there because he had once had his opportunity to go home to the States rich, and had not done it; had rather lost his wealth, and had then in his humiliation resolved to sever all communication with his home relatives and friends, and be to them thenceforth as one dead. Round about California in that day were scattered a host of these living dead men – pride-smitten poor fellows, grizzled and old at forty, whose secret thoughts were made all of regrets and longings – regrets for their wasted lives, and longings to be out of the struggle and done with it all.

It was a lonesome land! Not a sound in all those peaceful expanses of grass and woods but the drowsy hum of insects; no glimpse of man or beast; nothing to keep up your spirits and make you glad to be alive. And so, at last, in the early part of the afternoon, when I caught sight of a human creature, I felt a most grateful uplift. This person was a man about forty-five years old, and he was standing at the gate of one of those cozy little rose-clad cottages of the sort already referred to. However, this one hadn't a deserted look; it had the look of being lived in and petted and cared for and looked after; and so had its front yard, which was a garden of flowers, abundant, gay, and flourishing. I was invited in, of course, and required to make myself at home – it was the custom of the country.

It was delightful to be in such a place, after long weeks of daily and nightly familiarity with miners' cabins – with all which this implies of dirt floor, never-made beds, tin plates and cups, bacon and beans and black coffee, and nothing of ornament but war pictures from the Eastern illustrated papers tacked to the log walls. That was all hard, cheerless, materialistic desolation, but here was a nest which had aspects to rest the tired eye and refresh that something in one's nature which, after long fasting, recognizes, when

once: in the past.

to the States: to the eastern states of America.

had rather lost: instead he had lost. **wealth**: richness.

resolved: decided. **sever**: cut; stop. **home relatives**: members of his family who were at home. **thenceforth**: from that moment.

Round about: all around. **scattered**: dispersed.

host: great number. **pride-smitten**: damaged by their sense of honour. **fellows**: men. **grizzled**: with grey hair.

regrets: sense of repentance. **longings**: desires. **wasted**: not used well. **longings**: desires. **struggle**: laboured effort.

done with it all: having finished everything.

lonesome: solitary.

expanses: extensions; uninterrupted surfaces. **drowsy hum**: sleepy sound. **glimpse**: brief view. **to keep up**: console.

glad: happy. **at last**: in the end.

caught sight of: saw.

I felt a most grateful uplift: I felt considerably happier.

gate: external door. **cozy**: nice and friendly. **rose-clad**: covered with roses. **of the sort**: of the kind. **referred to**: described.

deserted look: abandoned aspect. **lived in**: inhabited. **petted**: loved.

gay: cheerful; merry.

flourishing: full of flowers. **of course**: naturally. **required**: asked. **to make myself at home**: to feel comfortable.

delightful: very pleasant. **in such a place**: a place like that; note the *construction*. **familiarity with**: being used to. **cabins**: poor and simple houses. **tin**: metal.

black coffee: coffee without milk.

but: except.

tacked: attached. **log**: trunk. **cheerless**: gloomy.

nest: cozy place.

fasting: period in which one doesn't eat.

confronted by the belongings of art, howsoever cheap and modest they may be, that it has unconsciously been famishing and now has found nourishment. I could not have believed that a rag carpet could feast me so, and so content me; or that there could be such solace to the soul in wallpaper and framed lithographs, and bright-colored tidies and lamp-mats, and Windsor chairs, and varnished what-nots, with sea-shells and books and china vases on them, and the score of little unclassifiable tricks and touches that a woman's hand distributes about a home, which one sees without knowing he sees them, yet would miss in a moment if they were taken away. The delight that was in my heart showed in my face, and the man saw it and was pleased; saw it so plainly that he answered it as if it had been spoken.

"All her work," he said, caressingly; "she did it all herself – every bit," and he took the room in with a glance which was full of affectionate worship. One of those soft Japanese fabrics with which women drape with careful negligence the upper part of a picture-frame was out of adjustment. He noticed it, and rearranged it with cautious pains, stepping back several times to gauge the effect before he got it to suit him. Then he gave it a light finishing pat or two with his hand, and said: "She always does that. You can't tell just what it lacks, but it does lack something until you've done that – you can see it yourself after it's done, but that is all you know; you can't find out the law of it. It's like the finishing pats a mother gives the child's hair after she's got it combed and brushed, I reckon. I've seen her fix all these things so much that I can do them all just her way, though I don't know the law of any of them. But she knows the law. She knows the why, and the how both; but I don't know the why; I only know the how."

He took me into a bedroom so that I might wash my hands;

belongings: possessions.

famishing: suffering from hunger.
rag carpet: not precious carpet. **feast me**: make me so happy.
solace: relief.
wallpaper: paper stuck to the wall. **framed**: put into frames.
tidies: small containers in which various articles are kept. **lamp-mats**: pieces of cloth kept under lamps. **what-nots**: things whose names are not important. **score**: great number.
tricks and touches: small details. **about**: around.

would miss: would feel their absence.
showed: was to be seen.
pleased: happy; satisfied. **plainly**: clearly.
spoken: said.
caressingly: with affection. **herself**: personally.
bit: small piece. **took the room in**: looked all about the room.
glance: look. **worship**: adoration.
fabrics: cloth. **drape**: cover.

out of adjustment: out of place. **pains**: cares.
stepping: walking. **several**: a lot of. **gauge**: measure.
to suit him: to be good for him. **light**: not hard. **pat**: slap; touch.

lacks: is missing.
yourself: personally.
law: rule.
pats: touches.
she's got it combed and brushed: she has combed and brushed it. **I reckon**: I think. **just**: exactly.
law: rule.
the why: the reason. **the how**: the system; the way.

such a bedroom as I had not seen for years: white counterpane, white pillows, carpeted floor, papered walls, pictures, dressing-table, with mirror and pin-cushion and dainty toilet things; and in the corner a wash-stand, with real china-ware bowl and pitcher, and with soap in a china dish, and on a rack more than a dozen towels – towels too clean and white for one out of practice to use without some vague sense of profanation. So my face spoke again, and he answered with gratified words:

"All her work; she did it all herself – every bit. Nothing here that hasn't felt the touch of her hand. Now you would think – But I mustn't talk so much."

By this time I was wiping my hands and glancing from detail to detail of the room's belongings, as one is apt to do when he is in a new place, where everything he sees is a comfort to his eye and his spirit; and I became conscious, in one of those unaccountable ways, you know, that there was something there somewhere that the man wanted me to discover for myself. I knew it perfectly, and I knew he was trying to help me by furtive indications with his eye, so I tried hard to get on the right track, being eager to gratify him. I failed several times, as I could see out of the corner of my eye without being told; but at last I knew I must be looking straight at the thing – knew it from the pleasure issuing in invisible waves from him. He broke into a happy laugh, and rubbed his hands together, and cried out:

"That's it! You've found it. I knew you would. It's her picture."

I went to the little black-walnut bracket on the farther wall, and did find there what I had not yet noticed – a daguerr-eotype-case. It contained the sweetest girlish face, and the most beautiful, as it seemed to me, that I had ever seen. The man drank the admiration from my face, and was fully

such a bedroom: note the construction with *such*.
counterpane: top cover on the bed.
dressing-table: small table with a mirror for cosmetics. **pin-cushion**: small cushion for pins and needles. **dainty**: elegant.
china-ware: article of porcelain. **bowl**: round container. **pitcher**:
container with a handle. **rack**: framework. **a dozen**: twelve. **towels**: pieces of cloth used for drying. **out of practice**: no more
used.
gratified: satisfied.
herself: personally. **bit**: small piece.

wiping: rubbing; drying. **glancing**: looking.
detail: particular. **belongings**: properties; objects. **apt**: likely.

spirit: soul.   **I became conscious**: I realized; I understood.
unaccountable: unexplainable.
somewhere: in some place. **wanted me to discover**: note the
infinitive construction after *want*. **for myself**: alone.

hard: with great energy. **to get on**: to find. **eager**: anxious.
failed: was wrong. **several**: a lot of.
at last: in the end.
I must be looking: *supposition in the past*. **straight**: directly.
issuing: coming.
broke into a happy laugh: laughed suddenly. **rubbed:** moved
one against the other.

picture: portrait.
black-walnut bracket: shelves of black wood.

daguerreotype: old form of photography. **girlish**: of a girl.

satisfied.

"Nineteen her last birthday," he said, as he put the picture back; "and that was the day we were married. When you see her – ah, just wait till you see her!"

"Where is she? When will she be in?"

"Oh, she's away now. She's gone to see her people. They live forty or fifty miles from here. She's been gone two weeks to-day."

"When do you expect her back?"

"This is Wednesday. She'll back Saturday, in the evening – about nine o'clock, likely."

I felt a sharp sense of disappointment.

"I'm sorry, because I'll be gone then, " I said, regretfully.

"Gone? No – why should you go? Don't go. She'll be so disappointed."

She would be disappointed – that beautiful creature! If she had said the words herself they could hardly have blessed me more. I was feeling a deep, strong longing to see her – a longing so supplicating, so insistent, that it made me afraid. I said to myself: "I will go straight away from this place, for my peace of mind's sake."

"You see, she likes to have people come and stop with us – people who know things, and can talk – people like you. She delights in it; for she knows – oh, she knows nearly everything herself, and can talk, oh, like a bird – and the books she reads, why, you would be astonished. Don't go; it's only a little while, you know, and she'll be so disappointed."

I heard the words, but hardly noticed them, I was so deep in my thinkings and strugglings. He left me, but I didn't know. Presently he was back, with the picture-case in his hand, and he held it open before me and said:

"There, now, tell her to her face you could have stayed to see her, and you wouldn't."

10

we were married: we bacame husband and wife.
just: only.
be in: be at home.
her people: her relatives.
she's been gone: she went.
two weeks to-day: two weeks ago.
expect her back: think she'll be back.
She'll back: she will be back.
likely: probably.
sharp: acute. **disappointment**: frustration.
regretfully: being very sorry.

disappointed: sorry.

herself: personally. **hardly**: with difficulty. **blessed**: pleased.
longing: desire.
made me afraid: scared me.
to myself: without speaking. **straight away**: immediately away.
for my peace of mind's sake: for the good of my peace of mind.

she delights in it: she likes it a lot. **nearly**: almost.

astonished: very surprised.
a little while: a short time.
disappointed: sorry; upset.
hardly: with difficulty.
deep in my thinkings and strugglings: strongly debated.
presently: immediately.
before me: in front of me.
to her face: directly.

That second glimpse broke down my good resolution. I would stay and take the risk. That night we smoked the tranquil pipe, and talked till late about various things, but mainly about her; and certainly I had had no such pleasant and restful time for many a day. The Thursday followed and slipped comfortably away. Toward twilight a big miner from three miles away came – one of the grizzled, stranded pioneers – and gave us warm salutation, clothed in grave and sober speech. Then he said:

"I only just dropped over to ask about the little madam, and when is she coming home. Any news from her?"

"Oh yes, a letter. Would you like to hear it, Tom?"

"Well, I should think I would, if you don't mind, Henry!"

Henry got the letter out of his wallet, and said he would skip some of the private phrases, if we were willing; then he went on and read the bulk of it – a loving, sedate, and altogether charming and gracious piece of handiwork, with a postscript full of affectionate regards and messages to Tom, and Joe, and Charley, and other close friends and neighbors.

As the reader finished, he glanced at Tom, and cried out: "Oho, you're at it again! Take your hands away, and let me see your eyes. You always do that when I read a letter from her. I will write and tell her.'

"Oh no, you mustn't, Henry. I'm getting old, you know, and any little disappointment makes me want to cry. I thought she'd be here herself, and now you've got only a letter."

"Well, now, what put that in your head? I thought everybody knew she wasn't coming till Saturday."

"Saturday! Why, come to think, I did know it. I wonder what's the matter with me lately? Certainly I knew it. Ain't we all getting ready for her? Well, I must be going now. But I'll be on hand when she comes, old man!"

glimpse: look. **broke down**: destroyed. **resolution**: decision.

tranquil pipe: pipe of peace.
mainly: most of all.
restful: tranquil; peaceful. **followed**: came.
slipped: passed. **twilight**: sunset.
miner: man working in a mine. **grizzled**: with grey hair.
stranded: worn out; consumed. **clothed**: covered.
grave: serious.
dropped over: came here. **madam**: lady.

don't mind: aren't sorry for that.
wallet: case for holding paper money and documents.
skip: avoid to read. **we were willing**: we allowed him.
went on: continued. **bulk**: content. **sedate**: calm.
altogether: as a whole. **charming**: pleasant. **handiwork**: work
produced by hand. **regards**: references; attentions.
close: intimate.
neighbors: (U.S.) neighbours; people living near.
glanced: looked
you're at it again: you are doing it again.

disappointment: frustration; sadness.
herself: personally.

she wasn't coming: *planned future* in the past.
come to think: now I remember. **I wonder**: I 'd like to know.
what's the matter: what's wrong. **lately**: recently.
Ain't we: *aren't we.* **I must be going**: I have to go.
on hand: present.

Late Friday afternoon another gray veteran tramped over from his cabin a mile or so away, and said the boys wanted to have a little gaiety and a good time Saturday night, if Henry thought she wouldn't be too tired after her journey to be kept up.

"Tired? She tired! Oh, hear the man! Joe, *you* know she'd sit up six weeks to please any one of you!"

When Joe heard that there was a letter, he asked to have it read, and the loving messages in it for him broke the old fellow all up; but he said he was such an old wreck *that* that would happen to him if she only just mentioned his name. "Lord, we miss her so!" he said.

Saturday afternoon I found I was taking out my watch pretty often. Henry noticed it, and said, with a startled look:

"You don't think she ought to be here so soon, do you?" I felt caught, and a little embarrassed; but I laughed, and said it was a habit of mine when I was in a state of expectancy. But he didn't seem quite satisfied; and from that time on he began to show uneasiness. Four times he walked me up the road to a point whence we could see a long distance; and there he would stand, shading his eyes with his hand, and looking. Several times he said:

"I'm getting worried, I'm getting right down worried. I know she's not due till about nine o'clock, and yet something seems to be trying to warn me that something's happened. You don't think anything has happened, do you?"

I began to get pretty thoroughly ashamed of him for his childishness; and at last, when he repeated that imploring question still another time, I lost my patience for the moment, and spoke pretty brutally to him. It seemed to shrivel him up and cow him; and he looked so wounded and so humble after that, that I detested myself for having

14

gray: with grey hair. **tramped**: came.
cabin: poor and simple house.
gaiety: feast.

to be kept up: to be kept out of bed; to be kept awake.

to please: to make happy.

to have it read: that he'd read it to him.
broke the old fellow all up: touched the old man. **wreck**: worn out man.
miss: feel her absence.

pretty: quite. **startled**: surprised.
look: aspect.
she ought to: she should.
caught: surprised.

quite: completely; very.
from that time on: starting from that moment. **uneasiness**: anxiety. **he walked me**: took me. **whence**: from where.
shading: protecting from the sun.
several: a lot of.
right down: very.
she's not due: she's not expected.
warn: advise.

do you?: *question tag*.
pretty thoroughly: very deeply.
childishness: behaving like a child. **at last**: in the end.

pretty: rather.
shrivel him up: move him. **cow him**: make him sad. **wounded**: hurt.

done the cruel and unnecessary thing. And so I was glad when Charley, another veteran, arrived toward the edge of the evening, and nestled up to Henry to hear the letter read, and talked over the preparations for the welcome. Charley fetched out one hearty speech after another, and did his best to drive away his friend's bodings and apprehensions. "Anything *happened* to her? Henry, that's pure nonsense. There isn't anything going to happen to her; just make your mind easy as to that. What did the letter say? Said she was well, didn't it? And said she'd be here by nine o'clock, didn't it? Did you ever know her to fail of her word? Why, you know you never did.Well, then, don't you fret; she'll *be* here, and that's absolutely certain, and as sure as you are born. Come, now, let's get to decorating – not much time left.

Pretty soon Tom and Joe arrived and then all hands set about adorning the house with flowers. Toward nine the three miners said that as they had brought their instruments they might as well tune up, for the boys and girls would soon be arriving now, and hungry for a good, oldfashioned break-down. A fiddle, a banjo, and a clarinet – these were the instruments. The trio took their places side by side, and began to play some rattling dancemusic, and beat time with their big boots.

It was getting very close to nine. Henry was standing in the door with his eyes directed up the road, his body swaying to the torture of his mental distress. He had been made to drink his wife's health and safety several times, and now Tom shouted:

"All hands stand by! One more drink, and she's here!"

Joe brought the glasses on a waiter, and served the party. I reached for one of the two remaining glasses, but Joe growled, under his breath:

"Drop that! Take the other."

glad: happy.
edge: beginning; margin.
nestled up to: stopped by.

fetched out: took out. **hearty**: friendly.
bodings: foreboding; feeling of a coming disaster.

make your mind easy: relax your mind.
by: not later than.
to fail of her word: not to keep her word.
fret: be afraid.

set about: started.

tune up: start playing. **would soon be arriving**: *future in the past*.
break-down: popular dance. **fiddle**: (informal) violin.
side by side: one next to the other.
rattling: very lively.

close to: near.
swaying: moving; swinging.
distress: anxiety.

stand by: be ready.
waiter: tray.
reached for: took.
growled: said in a low voice. **under his breath**: in a very low voice. **drop that**: leave that down.

Which I did. Henry was served last. He had hardly swallowed his drink when the clock began to strike. He listened till it finished, his face growing pale and paler; then he said:

"Boys, I'm sick with fear. Help me – I want to lie down!"

They helped him to the sofa. He began to nestle and drowse, but presently spoke like one talking in his sleep, and said: "Did I hear horses' feet? Have they come?"

One of the veterans answered, close to his ear: "It was Jimmy Parrish come to say the party got delayed, but they're right up the road a piece, and coming along. Her horse is lame, but she'll be here in half an hour."

"Oh, I'm *so* thankful nothing has happened!"

He was asleep almost before the words were out of his mouth. In a moment those handy men had his clothes off, and had tucked him into his bed in the chamber where I had washed my hands. They closed the door and came back. Then they seemed preparing to leave; but I said: "Please don't go, gentlemen. She won't know me; I am a stranger."

They glanced at each other. Then Joe said:

"She? Poor thing, she's been dead nineteen years!"

"Dead?"

"That or worse. She went to see her folks half a year after she was married, and on her way back, on a Saturday evening, the Indians captured her within five miles of this place, and she's never been heard of since."

"And he lost his mind in consequence?"

"Never has been sane an hour since. But he only gets bad when that time of the year comes round. Then we begin to drop in here, three days before she's due, to encourage him up, and ask if he's heard from her, and Saturday we all come and fix up the house with flowers, and get everything ready for a dance. We've done it every year for nineteen years. The first Saturday there was twenty-seven of us,

which: action which.

swallowed: drank. **strike**: strike the hours.

growing: getting; becoming. **pale and paler**: paler and paler.

I' m sick with fear: I'm terribly afraid.

to the sofa: to reach the sofa. **nestle**: be comfortable.

drowse: sleepy.

veterans: old miners. **close to**: near.

the party got delayed: the group of people coming were late.

a piece: at a short distance. **coming along**: arriving.

is lame: doesn't walk well.

handy: practical. **had his clothes off**: took off his clothes.

tucked him: put him.

seemed: appeared.

won't: will not.

glanced: looked.

she's been dead nineteen years: she died nineteen years ago

folks: parents.

on her way back: while she was coming back.

within: not farther than.

since: since that moment.

comes round: comes near.

drop in: come. **she's due**: she is supposed to come.

fix up: adorn.

get everything ready: prepare everything.

without counting the girls; there's only three of us now, and the girls are all gone. We drug him to sleep, or he would go wild; then he's all right for another year – thinks she's with him till the last three or four days come round; then he begins to look for her, and gets out his poor old letter, and we come and ask him to read it to us. Lord, she was a darling!"

[1893]

wild: crazy; furious.
come round: come near.
gets out: takes out.

darling: a very sweet girl.

The Notorious Jumping Frog of Calaveras County

In compliance with the request of a friend of mine, who wrote me from the East, I called on good-natured, garrulous old Simon Wheeler, and inquired after my friend's friend, Leonidas W. Smiley, as requested to do, and I hereunto append the result. I have a lurking suspicion that *Leonidas* W. Smiley is a myth; that my friend never knew such a personage; and that he only conjectured that if I asked old Wheeler about him, it would remind him of his infamous Jim Smiley, and he would go to work and bore me to death with some exasperating reminiscence of him as long and as tedious as it should be useless to me. If that was the design, it succeeded.

I found Simon Wheeler dozing comfortably by the barroom stove of the dilapidated tavern in the decayed mining camp of Angel's, and I noticed that he was fat and bald-headed, and had an expression of winning gentleness and simplicity upon his tranquil countenance. He roused up, and gave me good day. I told him that a friend of mine had commissioned me to make some inquiries about a cherished companion of his boyhood named *Leonidas* W. Smiley –*Rev. Leonidas* W. Smiley, a young minister of the Gospel, who he had heard was at one time a resident of Angel's Camp. I added that if Mr. Wheeler could tell me anything about this Rev. Leonidas W. Smiley, I would feel under many obligations to him.

Simon Wheeler backed me into a corner and blockaded me

Notorious: very famous for some bad quality. **Frog**: small amphibious animal, usually green. **Calaveras County**: county in North California, south east of Sacramento.

In compliance with: answering to.
East: East of U.S.A. **I called on**: I made a visit to. **garrulous**: loquacious; talkative. **inquired after**: asked about.
requested: asked.
hereunto: to this document. **append**: add. **lurking**: lingering and persistent.
conjectured: thought; imagined.
remind him: cause him to remember.
infamous: well-known for a bad quality. **go to work**: start. **bore**: tire. **reminiscence**: recollection.
tedious: boring. **useless**: of no utility.
design: project; purpose. **succeded**: worked.
dozing: sleeping lightly. **by**: near.
barroom: (U.S.) room where alcoholic drinks are served. **stove**: heating apparatus. **mining camp**: camp where minerals are extracted. **bald-headed**: with no hair on his head. **winning**: charming; attractive. **upon**: on. **countenance**: face. **roused up**: got up; stood up.
had commissioned me: had asked me. **inquiries**: researches.
cherished: very dear. **of his boyhood**: of when he was a boy.
Rev.: Reverend.
Gospel: New Testament. **at one time**: once; formerly.

I would feel under many obligations to him: I would feel very grateful to him.
backed me: let me move backwards. **blockaded**: blocked.

there with his chair, and then sat down and reeled off the monotonous narrative which follows this paragraph. He never smiled, he never frowned, he never changed his voice from the gentle-flowing key to which he tuned his initial sentence, he never betrayed the slightest suspicion of enthusiasm; but all through the interminable narrative there ran a vein of impressive earnestness and sincerity, which showed me plainly that, so far from his imagining that there was anything ridiculous or funny about his story, he regarded it as a really important matter, and admired its two heroes as men of transcendent genius in *finesse*. I let him go on in his own way, and never interrupted him once. "Rev. Leonidas W. H'm, Reverend Le – well, there was a feller here once by the name of *Jim* Smiley, in the winter of '49 – or maybe it was the spring of '50 – I don't recollect exactly, somehow, though what makes me think it was one or the other is because I remember the big flume warn't finished when he first come to the camp; but anyway, he was the curiousest man about always betting on anything that turned up you ever see, if he could get anybody to bet on the other side; and if he couldn't he'd change sides. Any way that suited the other man would suit *him* – any way just so's he got a bet, *he* was satisfied. But still he was lucky, uncommon lucky; he most always come out winner. He was always ready and laying for a chance; there couldn't be no solit'ry thing mentioned but that feller'd offer to bet on it, and take ary side you please, as I was just telling you. If there was a horse-race, you'd find him flush or you'd find him busted at the end of it; if there was a dog-fight, he'd bet on it; if there was a cat-fight, he'd bet on it; if there was a chicken-fight, he'd bet on it; why, if there was two birds setting on a fence, he would bet you which one would fly first; or if there was a camp-meeting, he would be there reg'lar to bet on Parson Walker, which he judged to be the

reeled off: recited.

narrative: story.

frowned: moved his forehead.

gentle-flowing key: tone which ran gently. **tuned**: adjusted the note of. **betrayed**: showed. **slightest**: smallest. **suspicion**: sign. **narrative**: story.

earnestness: seriousness.

plainly: clearly. **so far from**: very distant from.

funny: ridiculous.

regarded: considered. **matter**: question.

finesse: refinement.

go on: continue. **once**: one time.

Rev.: Reverend. **H'm**: interjection used to show hesitation.

feller: *fellow*; man. **by the name**: called.

recollect: remember.

though: even if.

flume: artificial channel. **warn't**: *wasn't*.

first: for the first time. **come**: *came*.

curiousest: strangest. **about**: in this place. **betting**: gambling; staking money. **turned up**: happened. **get**: find.

he'd: *he would*. **sides**: position; opinion.

suited: was good for.

just so's he got: *just so as he got*; only to be able to have. **still**: as a matter of fact. **come out winner**: resulted the winner.

laying for: waiting for. **chance**: opportunity.

no solit'ry thing: *no solitary thing*; not a single thing. **feller'd**: *fellow would*. **ary**: *any*. **side**: part. **please**: like; want.

horse-race: competition of horses. **flush**: (informal) with a lot of money. **busted**: bankrupt.

fence: enclosure. **bet you**: stake money with you.

camp-meeting: religious service in the open.

reg'lar: *regularly*. **Parson**: priest. **judged**: considered.

best exhorter about here, and so he was too, and a good man. If he even see a straddle-bug start to go anywheres, he would bet you how long it would take him to get to – to wherever he was going to, and if you took him up, he would foller that straddle-bug to Mexico but what he would find out where he was bound for and how long he was on the road. Lots of the boys here has seen that Smiley, and can tell you about him. Why, it never made no difference to *him* – he'd bet on *any* thing – the dangdest feller. Parson Walker's wife laid very sick once, for a good while, and it seemed as if they warn't going to save her; but one morning he come in, and Smiley up and asked him how she was, and he said she was considerable better – thank the Lord for his inf'nite mercy – and coming on so smart that with the blessing of Prov'dence she'd get well yet; and Smiley, before he thought, says, 'Well, I'll resk two-and-a-half she don't anyway.'

"Thish-yer Smiley had a mare – the boys called her the fifteen-minute nag, but that was only in fun, you know, because of course she was faster than that – and he used to win money on that horse, for all she was so slow and always had the asthma, or the distemper, or the consumption, or something of that kind. They used to give her two or three hundred yards' start and then pass her under way; but always at the fag end of the race she'd get excited and desperate like, and come cavorting and straddling up, and scattering her legs around limber, sometimes in the air, and sometimes out to one side among the fences, and kicking up m-o-r-e dust and raising m-o-r-e racket with her coughing and sneezing and blowing her nose – and *always* fetch up at the stand just about a neck ahead, as near as you could cipher it down.

"And he had a little small bull-pup, that to look at him you'd think he warn't worth a cent but to set around and

26

exhorter: persuader. **about**: around.

straddle-bug: long-legged insect. **anywheres**: to any place.

bet you: stake money with you. **to get to**: to reach.

took him up: accepted the bet.

foller: *follow*. **straddle-bug**: insect. **but what he would find out**: only to discover. **bound for**: directed to.

Lots of: a great number of. **has**: *have*.

dangdest feller: *damnedest fellow*.

laid very sick: was in bed very ill. **for a good while**: for quite a long time. **seemed**: appeared. **warn't**: *were not*.

come: *came*. **up**: (dialect) got up.

considerable: *considerably*.

inf'nite: *infinite*. **mercy**: pity. **coming on so smart**: recovering so quickly. **blessing**: protection and aid. **Prov'dence**: *Providence*.

says: *said*. **resk**: *risk*; bet.

she don't: *she doesn't*. **she don't anyway**: she will not recover.

Thish-yer Smiley: *this Smiley here*. **mare**: female horse.

nag: bad horse. **in fun**: as a joke.

faster: quicker.

for all: even if.

distemper: desease of animals.

consumption: respiratory desease. **kind**: sort; type.

to give her two or three hundred yards' start: to let her start two or three hundred yards ahead. **at the fag end**: at the very end.

race: competition. **cavorting**: jumping. **straddling**: spreading its legs. **scattering**: throwing in various directions. **limber**: in an agile way. **fences**: enclosures.

kicking up: throwing up with her legs. **dust**: powder. **racket**: noise. **coughing**: expelling air through its mouth. **sneezing**: expelling air through its nose. **fetch up**: (informal) arrived. **stand**: arrival point. **cipher it down**: count it.

bull-pup: young bulldog.

warn't worth: didn't have the value of. **but**: except. **set**: sit.

look ornery and lay for a chance to steal something. But as soon as money was up on him he was a different dog; his under-jaw'd begin to stick out like the fo'castle of a steamboat, and his teeth would uncover and shine like the furnaces. And a dog might tackle him and bully-rag him, and bite him, and throw him over his shoulder two or three times, and Andrew Jackson – which was the name of the pup – Andrew Jackson would never let on but what *he* was satisfied, and hadn't expected nothing else – and the bets being doubled and doubled on the other side all the time, till the money was all up; and then all of a sudden he would grab that other dog jest by the j'int of his hind leg and freeze to it – not chaw, you understand, but only just grip and hang on till they throwed up the sponge, if it was a year. Smiley always come out winner on that pup, till he harnessed a dog once that didn't have no hind legs, because they'd been sawed off in a circular saw, and when the thing had gone along far enough and the money was all up, and he come to make a snatch for his pet holt, he see in a minute how he'd been imposed on, and how the other dog had him in the door, so to speak, and he 'peared surprised, and then he looked sorter discouraged-like, and didn't try no more to win the fight, and so he got shucked out bad. He give Smiley a look, as much as to say his heart was broke, and it was *his* fault, for putting up a dog that hadn't no hind legs for him to take holt of, which was his main dependence in a fight, and then he limped off a piece and laid down and died. It was a good pup, was that Andrew Jackson, and would have made a name for hisself if he'd lived, for the stuff was in him and he had genius – I know it, because he hadn't no opportunities to speak of, and it don't stand to reason that a dog could make such a fight as he could under them circumstances if he hadn't no talent. It always makes me feel sorry when I think of that last fight of his'n, and

look ornery: (U.S. dialect) have a vile-tempered aspect. **steal**: take away. **was up**: was bet.

under-jaw: lower part of the head. **stick out**: come out. **fo'castle**: *forecastle*; upper deck of a ship. **uncover**: be shown. **shine**: reflect light. **tackle**: challange. **bully-rag**: intimidate. **bite**: grip with its teeth.

pup: young dog. **never let on but what**: allow only what. **bets**: money at stake.
all the time: continuously.
was all up: had all been bet.
grab: seize; catch. **jest**: *just*; exactly. **j'int**: joint; middle. **hind**: posterior. **freeze to it**: take it firmly. **chaw**: *chew*. Keep in the mouth without swallowing. **hang on**: resist. **throwed**: *threw*. **come**: *came*. **pup**: dog.

harnessed: met. **didn't have no**: *had no*. In formal English the *double negative* is not used. **saw**: tool for cutting wood. **had gone along far enough**: had lasted enough. **all up:** all bet. **to make a snatch for**: to try. **his pet holt**: his favourite hold. **imposed on**: deceived.

had him in the door: had defeated him. **'peared**: *appeared*.
sorter: *sort of*; rather. **didn't try no more**: *tried no more*. **he got shucked out bad**: (U.S. informal) he had been defeated. **was broke**: *was broken*.
putting up: providing; supplying. **hadn't no**: *had no*. **hind**: posterior. **to take holt of**: to seize. **main dependence**: principal confidence. **limped off**: walked feebly away. **a piece**: (U.S.) a short distance. **pup**: dog.
made a name for hisself: became famous. **hisself**: *himself*.

hadn't no: *had no*. **it don't**: *it doesn't*.
it don't stand to reason: it is inconceivable.
them: *those*. **hadn't no**: *had no*.
his'n: *his*.

the way it turned out.

"Well, thish-yer Smiley had rat-tarriers, and chicken cocks, and tomcats and all them kind of things, till you couldn't rest, and you couldn't fetch nothing for him to bet on but he'd match you. He ketched a frog one day, and took him home, and said he cal'lated to educate him; and so he never done nothing for three months but set in his back yard and learn that frog to jump. And you bet you he *did* learn him, too. He'd give him a little punch behind, and the next minute you'd see that frog whirling in the air like a doughnut – see him turn one summerset, or maybe a couple, if he got a good start, and come down flat-footed and all right, like a cat. He got him up so in the matter of ketching flies, and kep' him in practice so constant, that he'd nail a fly every time as fur as he could see him. Smiley said all a frog wanted was education, and he could do 'most anything – and I believe him. Why, I've seen him set Dan'l Webster down here on this floor – Dan'l Webster was the name of the frog – and sing out, 'Flies, Dan'l, flies!' and quicker'n you could wink he'd spring straight up and snake a fly off'n the counter there, and flop down on the floor ag'in as solid as a gob of mud, and fall to scratching the side of his head with his hind foot as indifferent as if he hadn't no idea he'd been doin' any more'n any frog might do. You never see a frog so modest and straightfor'ard as he was, for all he was so gifted. And when it come to fair and square jumping on a dead level, he could get over more ground at one straddle than any animal of his breed you ever see. Jumping on a dead level was his strong suit, you understand; and when it come to that, Smiley would ante up money on him as long as he had a red. Smiley was monstrous proud of his frog, and well he might be, for fellers that had traveled and been everywheres all said he laid over any frog that ever *they* see.

turned out: finished.

thish-yer: *this here* (U.S. not standard).   **rat-tarriers**: dogs trained to catch rats. **tomcats**: male cats. **them**: *those*.

rest: pause. **fetch**: find. **couldn't fetch nothing**: *could fetch nothing*. **match you**: bet with you. **ketched**: *caught*.

cal'lated: *calculated*; had in mind. **him**: the frog.

he never done nothing… but: *he did nothing apart from*.

learn: *here* teach. **did**: *to do* gives *emotive emphasis*.

punch: blow; stroke.

whirling: turning.

doughnut: small ringshaped fried cake. **summerset**: somersault; achrobatic roll. **come**: *came*.

he got him up so: he trained it.

ketching: *catching* . **flies**: insects. **kep'**: *kept*. **him**: the frog. **in practice**: in exercise. **nail**: catch. **as fur as**: *as far as*. **him**: it (the fly). **wanted**: needed. **'most**: *almost*.

Why: *because*. Why has an interrogative meaning. **set**: place. **Dan'l**: Daniel.

sing out: sing in a loud voice.

quicker'n: *quicker than*.   **wink**: close and open your eyes.

snake: catch. **off'n**: *off of*. **counter**: table where food and drinks are served. **ag'in**: *again*. **gob of mud**: lump, piece of wet soil. **fall to**: begin; start. **hind**: posterior.

hadn't no: *had no*. **more'n**: *more than*.

straightfor'ard: *straightforward*; direct.

he: it (the frog). **he was so gifted**: it had such natural abilities.

dead level: plain surface.

straddle: jump. **breed**: kind.

dead level: plain surface. **his strong suit**: its main ability.

would ante up: would bet.

on him: on it (on his frog). **a red**: a cent.

monstrous proud: greatly satisfied. **well he might be**: he was right to be. **fellers**: *fellows*; people. **everywheres**: in every place. **laid over**: was better than. **ever *they* see**: *they had ever seen*.

"Well, Smiley kep' the beast in a little lattice box, and he used to fetch him down-town sometimes and lay for a bet. One day a feller – a stranger in the camp, he was – come acrost him with his box, and says:

"'What might it be that you've got in the box?'

"And Smiley says, sorter indifferent-like, 'It might be a parrot, or it might be a canary, maybe, but it ain't – it's only just a frog.'

"And the feller took it, and looked at it careful, and turned it round this way and that, and says, 'H'm - so 'tis. Well, what's *he* good for?'

"'Well,' Smiley says, easy and careless, 'he's good enough for *one* thing, I should judge – he can outjump any frog in Calaveras County.'

"The feller took the box again, and took another long, particular look, and give it back to Smiley, and says, very deliberate, 'Well,' he says, 'I don't see no p'ints about that frog that's any better'n any other frog.'

"'Maybe you don't,' Smiley says. 'Maybe you understand frogs and maybe you don't understand 'em; maybe you've had experience, and maybe you ain't only a amature, as it were. Anyways, I've got *my* opinion, and I'll resk forty dollars that he can outjump any frog in Calaveras County.'

"And the feller studied a minute, and then says, kinder sad-like, 'Well, I'm only a stranger here, and I ain't got no frog; but if I had a frog, I'd bet you.'

"And then Smiley says, 'That's all right – that's all right – if you'll hold my box a minute, I'll go and get you a frog.' And so the feller took the box, and put up his forty dollars along with Smiley's, and set down to wait.

"So he set there a good while thinking and thinking to himself, and then he got the frog out and prized his mouth open and took a teaspoon and filled him full of quail-shot – filled him pretty near up to his chin – and set him on the

kep': *kept*. **lattice box**: box of strips of wood or metal.

fetch: take. **down-town**: to the centre of the town.

feller: *fellow*; man. **stranger in the camp**: not known in the camp. **come acrost him**: *came across him*; met him by chance.

says: said. **sorter**: *sort of*; rather. **indifferent-like**: looking indifferent. **parrot**: tropical bird. **ain't**: *isn't*.

only just: only.

feller: *fellow*. **careful**: *carefully*; with attention.

this way and that: everywhere. **says**: said. **H'm**: exclamation of doubt. **'tis**: *it is*. **what's *he* good for?**: what can it do?.

says: *said*. **easy and careless**: in a very relaxed way.

I should judge: I suppose. **outjump**: jump higher than.

Calaveras County: county in California.

feller: *fellow*; man.

took...a look: looked at it. **give**: *gave*. **says**: *said*.

deliberate: deliberately; carefully. **I don't see no p'ints**: *I see no points*. **better'n**: *better than*.

says: *said*.

'em: *them*.

ain't: *aren't*. **a amature**: *an amateur*; not a professional.

resk: *risk*.

outjump: jump higher than.

feller: *fellow*; man. **studied**: thought. **says**: *said*. **kinder**: *kind of*; rather. **sad-like**: in a sad way. **ain't got no frog**: *have no frog*.

says: *said*. **That's all right**: it's o.k.

if you'll hold: if you keep in your hands. The *future tense* used in an *if-clause* is very informal. **feller**: *fellow*; man.

along with: together with. **set**: *sat*.

a good while: for quite a long time.

to himself: in his own mind. **prized**: opened with force.

filled him full of: *filled it with*. **quail-shot**: very little stones.

pretty near up to: almost to. **set him**: placed it (the frog).

floor. Smiley he went to the swamp and slopped around in the mud for a long time, and finally he ketched a frog, and fetched him in, and give him to this feller, and says:

"'Now, if you're ready, set him alongside of Dan'l, with his fore paws just even with Dan'l's, and I'll give the word. ' Then he says, 'One – two – three – *git!*' and him and the feller touched up the frogs from behind, and the new frog hopped off lively, but Dan'l give a heave, and hysted up his shoulders – so – like a Frenchman, but it warn't no use – he couldn't budge; he was planted as solid as a church, and he couldn't no more stir than if he was anchored out. Smiley was a good deal surprised, and he was disgusted too, but he didn't have no idea what the matter was, of course.

"The feller took the money and started away; and when he was going out at the door, he sorter jerked his thumb over his shoulder – so – at Dan'l, and says again, very deliberate, 'Well,' he says, '*I* don't see no p'ints about that frog that's any better'n any other frog.'

"Smiley he stood scratching his head and looking down at Dan'l a long time, and at last he says, 'I do wonder what in the nation that frog throw'd off for – I wonder if there ain't something the matter with him – he 'pears to look mighty baggy, somehow.' And he ketched Dan'l by the nap of the neck, and hefted him, and says, 'Why blame my cats if he don't weigh five pound!' and turned him upside down and he belched out a double handful of shot. And then he see how it was, and he was the maddest man – he set the frog down and took out after that feller, but he never ketched him. And –"

[Here Simon Wheeler heard his name called from the front yard, and got up to see what was wanted.] And turning to me as he moved away, he said: "Just set where you are, stranger, and rest easy – I ain't going to be gone a second."

Smiley he: the repetition of the subject is *very informal*. **swamp**: marsh; bog. **mud**: wet soil. **ketched**: caught.

feller: *fellow*; man. **says**: *said*.

set him alongside of: place it near. **Dan'l**: Daniel.

fore paws: front legs. **just even**: exactly on the same line. **I'll give the word**: I will say "go". *git!*: *go!*

feller: *fellow*; man.

hopped off: jumped off. **give a heave**: tried to jump. **hysted up**: raised; lifted. **warn't no use**: *was of no use*.

budge: move.

he couldn't no more: *he could no more*. **stir**: move. **anchored out**: fixed with an anchor. **a good deal**: very.

he didn't have no idea: *he had no idea*. **matter**: reason.

feller: *fellow*; man. **started away**: started to go away.

out at (very informal) out of. **sorter**: *sort of*. **jerked his thumb**: pointed. **says**: *said*.

deliberate: deliberately; intentionally. **I don't see no**: *I see no*.

p'ints: *points*. **better'n**: *better than*.

Smiley he: *very informal*. **stood**: didn't move.

at last: finally. **I do wonder**: I am very surprised. *Do* here is used with emphatic meaning. **what in the nation**: why. **throw'd off**: gave up; renounced. **ain't**: *isn't*. **the matter**: wrong. **'pears**: *appears*; seems. **mighty baggy**: very swallen. **ketched**: *caught*. **nap**: skin. **hefted**: raised; lifted. **says**: *said*. **Why blame my cats**: exclamation of surprise. **he don't**: *he doesn't*.

upside down: with the feet up and the head down. **belched out**: expelled. **see**: *saw*. **maddest**: most angry.

took out after: followed. **feller**: *fellow*; man.

ketched: *caught*.

heard his name called: note the construction with *to hear*.

moved away: went away. **set**: *stay*.

I ain't going to be gone a second: (dialect) I'll be right back.

But, by your leave, I did not think that a continuation of the history of the enterprising vagabond *Jim* Smiley would be likely to afford me much information concerning the Rev. *Leonidas W.* Smiley, and so I started away.

At the door I met the sociable Wheeler returning, and he buttonholed me and recommenced:

"Well, thish-yer Smiley had a yaller one-eyed cow that didn't have no tail, only just a short stump like a bannanner, and –"

However, lacking both time and inclination, I did not wait to hear about the afflicted cow, but took my leave.

[1875]

by your leave: (addressed to the reader) if you allow me.

enterprising: ready for adventures.

likely: probable. **afford**: give. **much information**: note that *information* is always singular. **I started away**: I went away.

sociable: friendly.

buttonholed me: stopped me to talk.

thish-yer: this here (U.S. informal). **yaller:** *yellow*.

didn't have no tail: *had no tail*. **stump**: short and fat piece.

bannanner: *banana*.

lacking: not having. **inclination**: good disposition.

afflicted: injured. **took my leave**: went away.

Journalism in Tennessee

The editor of the Memphis *Avalanche* swoops thus mildly down upon a correspondent who posted him as a Radical: – "While he was writing the first word, the middle, dotting his i's, crossing his t's and punching his period, he knew he was concocting a sentence that was saturated with infamy and reeking with falsehood."

Exchange

I was told by the physician that a Southern climate would improve my health, and so I went down to Tennessee, and got a berth on the *Morning Glory and Johnson County War-Whoop* as associate editor. When I went on duty I found the chief editor sitting tilted back in a three-legged chair with his feet on a pine table. There was another pine table in the room and another afflicted chair, and both were half buried under newspapers and scraps and sheets of manuscript. There was a wooden box of sand, sprinkled with cigar stubs and "old soldiers," and a stove with a door hanging by its upper hinge. The chief editor had a long-tailed black cloth frock-coat on, and white linen pants. His boots were small and neatly blacked. He wore a ruffled shirt, a large seal-ring, a standing collar of obsolete pattern, and checkered neckerchief with the ends hanging down. Date of costume about 1848. He was smoking a cigar, and trying to think of a word, and in pawing his hair he had rumpled his locks a good deal. He was scowling fearfully, and I judged that he was concocting a particular-

editor: person in charge of the editing and the policy of a newspaper. **swoops thus mildly down upon**: attacks gently in this way.

dotting: writing a dot, a small point. **crossing**: writing the horizontal line of. **punching**: writing the fullstops. **concocting**: building up; constructing. **saturated with**: full of. **reeking**: smelling badly. *Exchange*: name of a newspaper.

I was told: note the *passive construction*. **physician**: doctor.
improve: make better. **health**: physical condition.
got a berth on: (informal, nautical) had a job at.
associate editor: subordinate editor. **on duty**: to work.
chief editor: most important editor. **tilted back**: leaning backward.
afflicted: broken.
buried: submerged; covered. **scraps**: pieces of papers.
sprinkled: scattered; not fully covered.
cigar stubs: pieces of cigars. **"old soldiers"**: chewed pieces of tobacco. **upper**: superior. **hinge**: device for holding together two parts. **frock-coat**: man's coat worn in the XIX century. **linen pants**: (U.S.) trousers of a hard-wearing fabric. **neatly**: accurately. **ruffled shirt**: wrinkled shirt. **seal-ring**: finger ring with a seal on it. **checkered**: (U.S.) chequered; with squares of different colours. **costume**: style of dressing.
pawing: (informal) touching in a rough way.
rumpled: ruffled. **locks**: curls. **a good deal**: a lot. **scowling**: contracting his brows. **concocting**: creating.

ly knotty editorial. He told me to take the exchanges and skim through them and write up the "Spirit of the Tennessee Press," condensing into the article all of their contents that seemed of interest.

I wrote as follows:

SPIRIT OF THE TENNESSEE PRESS

The editors of the Semi-Weekly Earthquake *evidently labor under a misapprehension with regard to the Bally-hack railroad. It is not the object of the company to leave Buzzardville off to one side. On the contrary, they consider it one of the most important points along the line, and consequently can have no desire to slight it. The gentlemen of the* Earthquake *will, of course, take pleasure in making the correction.*

John W. Blossom, Esq., the able editor of the Higginsville Thunderbolt and Battle Cry of Freedom, *arrived in the city yesterday. He is stopping at the Van Buren House.*

We observe that our contemporary of the Mud Springs Morning Howl *has fallen into the error of supposing that the election of Van Werter is not an established fact, but he will have discovered his mistake before this reminder reaches him, no doubt. He was doubtless misled by incomplete election returns.*

It is pleasant to note that the city of Blathersville is endeavoring to contract with some New York gentlemen to pave its well-nigh impassable streets with the Nicholson pavement. The Daily Hurrah *urges the measure with ability, and seems confident of ultimate success.*

I passed my manuscript over to the chief editor for acceptance, alteration, or destruction. He glanced at it and his face clouded. He ran his eye down the pages, and his

knotty: difficult; complicated. **editorial**: article written by the editor. **skim through**: look quickly through. **write up**: write summing up. **Press**: journalism.
all of their contents: all what they said. **seemed**: appeared.
as follows: as you find here below.

PRESS: journalism.

editors: persons in charge of the editing and of the policy of a newspaper. *labor*: work. *misapprehension*: a failure in under-standing properly. *railroad*: (U.S.) railway. *object*: purpose.
to leave Buzzardville off to one side: not to include Buzzardvil-le.
can have no desire : it is not possible that they want. *to slight*: (U.S.) not pay adequate attention to. *take pleasure in*: be glad to.

Esq.: Esquire; title of respect.
Thunderbolt: flash of lightning after a thunder. *arrived in:* note that *arrive* is followed by *in* or *at*. *He is stopping*: *planned future.*
contemporary: member of a rival newspaper.
supposing: thinking.
established fact: secure, certain fact.
mistake: error. *reminder*: note to remind.
doubtless: certainly; without any doubt. *misled*: taken into error.
election returns: statements of the votes counted in the election.

endeavoring: trying with an effort. *pave*: to cover with a solid surface. *well-nigh impassable*: on which is almost impossible to pass. *pavement*: solid surface. *urges*: insists on.
confident: sure. *ultimate*: final.

passed my manuscript over: gave my manuscript.
alteration: changes. **glanced at it**: looked shortly at it.
clouded: became dark.

countenance grew portentous. It was easy to see that something was wrong. Presently he sprang up and said: "Thunder and lighting! Do you suppose I am going to speak of those cattle that way? Do you suppose my subscribers are going to stand such gruel as that? Give me the pen!"

I never saw a pen scrape and scratch its way so viciously, or plow through another man's verbs and adjectives so relentlessly. While he was in the midst of his work, somebody shot at him through the open window, and marred the symmetry of my ear.

"Ah," said he, "that is that scoundrel Smith, of the *Moral Volcano* – he was due yesterday." And he snatched a navy revolver from his belt and fired. Smith dropped, shot in the thigh. The shot spoiled Smith's aim, who was just taking a second chance, and he crippled a stranger. It was me. Merely a finger shot off.

Then the chief editor went on with his erasures and interlineations. Just as he finished them a hand-grenade came down the stove-pipe, and the explosion shivered the stove into a thousand fragments. However, it did no further damage, except that a vagrant piece knocked a couple of my teeth out.

"That stove is utterly ruined," said the chief editor.

I said I believed it was.

"Well, no matter – don't want it this kind of weather. I know the man that did it. I'll get him. Now, *here* is the way this stuff ought to be written."

I took the manuscript. It was scarred with erasures and interlineations till its mother wouldn't have known it if it had had one. It now read as follows:

countenance: face. **grew portentous**: bacame of evil signifi-
cance. **Presently**: suddenly. **sprang up**: stood up
Thunder and lighting: exclamation of strong surprise.
cattle: animals. **that way**: in that manner.
my subscribers: the people who regularly pay for my newspaper. **gruel**: (informal) bore; uninteresting thing.
scrape and scratch: grate; rub. **viciously**: cruelly.
plow: (U.S.) plough; turn the ground.
relentlessly: without any pity. **midst**: middle.
shot at him: fired at him.
marred: disfigured; ruined.
scoundrel: wicked person.
was due: was expected. **snatched**: took.
navy revolver: revolver used in the navy. **fired**: shot. **dropped**:
fell down. **thigh**: upper part of the leg. **aim**: direction of the shot.
chance: opportunity. **crippled**: disabled; mutilated.
Merely: only.
went on: continued. **erasures**: cancellations.
interlineations: writing through the lines. **Just as**: in the moment
when. **stove-pipe**: tube of the heating apparatus. **shivered**:
destroyed.
further: other. **vagrant**: without a fixed direction.

stove: heating apparatus. **utterly**: definitely.

no matter: it isn't important. **weather**: climate.
I'll get him: I'll take him.
stuff: thing. **ought to**: should.
scarred: marked. **erasures**: cancellations.
interlineations: writing through the lines. **till**: in such a way that.
read as follows: was in this way.

The inveterate liars of the Semi-Weekly Earth-quake *are evidently endeavoring to palm off upon a noble and chivalrous people another of their vile and brutal falsehoods with regard to that most glorious conception of the nineteenth century, the Ballyhack railroad. The idea that Buzzardville was to be left off at one side originated in their own fulsome brains – or rather in the settlings which they regard as brains. They had better swallow this lie if they want to save their abandoned reptile carcasses the cowhiding they so richly deserve.*

That ass, Blossom, of the Higginsville Thunderbolt and Battle Cry of Freedom, *is down here again sponging at the Van Buren.*

We observe that the besotted blackguard of the Mud Springs Morning Howl *is giving out, with his usual propensity for lying, that Van Werter is not elected. The heaven-born mission of journalism is to disseminate truth; to eradicate error; to educate, refine, and elevate the tone of public morals and manners, and make all men more gentle, more virtuous, more charitable, and in all ways better, and holier, and happier; and yet this black-hearted scoundrel degrades his great office persistently to the dissemination of falsehood, calumny, vituperation, and vulgarity.*

Blathersville wants a Nicholson pavement – it wants a jail and a poor-house more. The idea of a pavement in a one-horse town composed of two gin-mills, a blacksmith shop, and that mustard-plaster of a newspaper, the Daily Hurrah! *The crawling insect, Buckner, who edits the* Hurrah, *is braying about his business with his customary imbecility, and imagining that he is talking sense.*

"Now *that* is the way to write – peppery and to the point.

inverterate : long-established. *liars*: persons who don't tell the truth. *endeavoring*: trying. *to palm off*: turn.

chivalrous: gallant; courteous.

falsehoods: falsities; lies. *most*: very. *conception*: design; product. *railroad*: (U.S.) railway.

left off at one side: not included.

fulsome: insincere. *brains*: minds. *settlings*: sediments.

regard as: consider. *swallow*: ingurgitate.

lie: insincerity. *save*: avoid. *reptile carcasses*: insignificant bodies. *cowhiding*: strokes of whip. *deserve*: have the right to have. *ass*: stupid animal.

sponging at: absorbing money from.

besotted: foolish; stupid. *blackguard*: less important members.

giving out: publishing.

lying: being insincere.

heaven-born: divine.

eradicate: cancel completely. *refine*: make better.

charitable: generous.

holier: more virtuous. *black-hearted*: with a black, evil heart.

scoundrel: very vile and bad man. *persistently*: continuously.

falsehood: falsity. *vituperation*: abusive, offensive language.

wants: needs. *pavement*: solid covering of the road. *jail*: prison.

poor-house: public institution offering accommodation to the poor. *one-horse*: small. *gin-mills*: taverns. *blacksmith*: artisan who works iron. *mustard-plaster*: oinment made of mustard seeds. *crawling*: moving on the ground. *edits*: is in charge of. *braying:* shouting like a donkey. *customary*: usual.

talking sense: saying something intelligent.

peppery: sharply. *to the point*: directly.

Mush-and-milk journalism gives me the fantods."

About this time a brick came through the window with a splintering crash, and gave me a considerable of a jolt in the back. I moved out of range – I began to feel in the way. The chief said, "That was the Colonel, likely. I've been expecting him for two days. He will be up now right away."

He was correct. The Colonel appeared in the door a moment afterward with a dragoon revolver in his hand. He said, "Sir, have I the honor of addressing the poltroon who edits this mangy sheet?"

"You have. Be seated, sir. Be careful of the chair, one of its legs is gone. I believe I have the honor of addressing the putrid liar, Colonel Blatherskite Tecumseh?"

"Right, sir. I have a little account to settle with you. If you are at leisure we will begin."

"I have an article on the 'Encouraging Progress of Moral and Intellectual Development in America' to finish, but there is no hurry. Begin.''

Both pistols rang out their fierce clamor at the same instant. The chief lost a lock of his hair, and the Colonel's bullet ended its career in the fleshy part of my thigh. The Colonel's left shoulder was clipped a little. They fired again. Both missed their men this time, but I got my share, a shot in the arm. At the third fire both gentlemen were wounded slightly, and I had a knuckle chipped. I then said, I believed I would go out and take a walk, as this was a private matter, and I had a delicacy about participating in it further. But both gentlemen begged me to keep my seat, and assured me that I was not in the way.

They then talked about the elections and the crops while they reloaded, and I fell to tying up my wounds. But presently they opened fire again with animation, and every shot took effect – but it is proper to remark that five out of

46

mush-and-milk: *here* sentimental.   **gives me the fantods**: makes me uneasy. **brick**: rectangular block used in the construction of walls. **splintering**: breaking into small fragments. **jolt**: stroke. **out of range**: to a place that couldn't be reached. **likely**: probably.

I've been expecting: *duration form*. **will be up**: will appear. **right away**: immediately.

dragoon revolver: revolver used by the cavalry.

honor: (U.S.) honour.   **poltroon**: coward.

edits: directs.   **mangy sheet**: very bad newspaper.

Be seated: sit down. **careful**: prudent.

putrid liar: rotten man who tells lies.

Right: exact.   **to settle**: to arrange.

are at leisure: have time and good disposition.

Development: progress; growth.

hurry: haste.

rang out: emitted.   **fierce clamor**: loud noise.

lock: curl.

bullet: projectile.   **career**: run.   **fleshy**: with flesh; soft. **thigh**: upper part of the leg. **clipped**: cut; slightly injured. **fired**: shot.

missed: didn't reach.   **share**: part.

shot: projectile; stroke.   **fire**: shot.

wounded: injured.   **slightly**: a little. **knuckle**: joint of the finger.

believed: thought. **take a walk**: walk for a while.

matter: question. **I had a delicacy about**: I didn't find polite.

begged: asked. t**o keep my seat**: to stay there.

in the way: in their line of fire.

crops: production of cultivations.

reloaded: charged again.   **I fell to tying up**: I began to bind securely. **presently**: in that moment.

proper: right. **remark**: observe.

the six fell to my share. The sixth one mortally wounded the Colonel, who remarked, with fine humor, that he would have to say good morning now, as he had business uptown. He then inquired the way to the undertaker's and left.

The chief turned to me and said, "I am expecting company to dinner, and shall have to get ready. It will be a favor to me if you will read proof and attend to the customers."

I winced a little at the idea of attending to the customers, but I was too bewildered by the fusillade that was still ringing in my ears to think of anything to say.

He continued, "Jones will be here at three – cowhide him. Gillespie will call earlier, perhaps – throw him out of the window. Ferguson will be along about four – kill him. That is all for to-day, I believe. If you have any odd time, you may write a blistering article on the police – give the chief inspector rats. The cowhides are under the table; weapons in the drawer – ammunition there in the corner – lint, and bandages up there in the pigeonholes. In case of accident, go to Lancet, the surgeon, down-stairs. He advertises – we take it out in trade."

He was gone. I shuddered. At the end of the next three hours I had been through perils so awful that all peace of mind and all cheerfulness were gone from me. Gillespie had called and thrown *me* out of the window. Jones arrived promptly, and when I got ready to do the cowhiding he took the job off my hands. In an encounter with a stranger, not in the bill of fare, I had lost my scalp. Another stranger, by the name of Thompson, left me a mere wreck and ruin of chaotic rags. And at last, at bay in the corner, and beset by an infuriated mob of editors, blacklegs, politicians, and desperadoes, who raved and swore and flourished their weapons about my head till the air shimmered with glancing flashes of steel, I was in the act of resigning my

fell to my share: reached me. **wounded**: injured.

remarked: observed. **fine**: subtle.

business: something to do.

uptown: in the upper part of the town. **inquired**: asked. **undertaker**: person who buried the dead. **left**: went away.

I am expecting: *planned future*.

favor: (U.S.) favour.

read proof: correct the printed errors. **attend to**: take care of.

winced: startled. **customers**: people who bought the paper.

bewildered: shocked.

ringing: resounding.

cowhide him: strike him with a whip.

will call: will come here.

will be along: will be here.

I believe: I guess; I think. **odd time**: time left.

blistering: sharp.

give the chief inspector rats: give the chief inspector a hard time.

lint: cotton. **pigeonholes**: small compartments for papers, letters, etc. **surgeon**: doctor.

advertises: publishes his advertisments. **we take it out in trade**: we don't make him pay. **shuddered**: trembled.

perils: dangers. **awful**: terrible.

cheerfulness: happiness; gaiety.

called: came.

to do the cowhiding: to strike him with a whip.

off: away from. **encounter**: meeting.

bill of fare: menu. **not in the bill of fare**: in an unforeseen way.

a mere wreck: a pure ruin.

rags: small pieces of cloth. **at last**: finally. **at bay**: unable to move. **mob**: disorderly crowd. **blacklegs**: cheaters.

raved: spoke in an uncontrolled manner. **flourished**: moved in the air. **weapons**: arms. **shimmered**: reflected light.

steel: very hard metal.

berth on the paper when the chief arrived, and with him a rabble of charmed and enthusiastic friends. Then ensued a scene of riot and carnage such as no human pen, or steel one either, could describe. People were shot, probed, dismembered, blown up, thrown out of the window. There was a brief tornado of murky blasphemy, with a confused and frantic war-dance glimmering through it, and then all was over. In five minutes there was silence, and the gory chief and I sat alone and surveyed the sanguinary ruin that strewed the floor around us.

He said, "You'll like this place when you get used to it." I said, "I'll have to get you to excuse me; I think maybe I might write to suit you after a while; as soon as I had had some practice and learned the language I am confident I could. But, to speak the plain truth, that sort of energy of expression has its inconveniences, and a man is liable to interruption. You see that yourself. Vigorous writing is calculated to elevate the public, no doubt, but then I do not like to attract so much attention as it calls forth. I can't write with comfort when I am interrupted so much as I have been to-day. I like this berth well enough, but I don't like to be left here to wait on the customers. The experiences are novel, I grant you, and entertaining, too, after a fashion, but they are not judiciously distributed. A gentleman shoots at you through the window and cripples *me*; a bombshell comes down the stove-pipe for your gratification and sends the stove door down *my* throat; a friend drops in to swap compliments with you, and freckles *me* with bullet-holes till my skin won't hold my principles; you go to dinner, and Jones comes with his cowhide, Gillespie throws me out of the window, Thompson tears all my clothes off, and an entire stranger takes my scalp with the easy freedom of an old acquaintance; and in less than five minutes all the blackguards in the country arrive

resigning my berth on: leaving my job at.

rabble: a disorderly crowd.   **charmed**: delighted.   **ensued**: followed.   **riot**: tumult.

shot: fired.   **probed**: penetrated with a sharp weapon.

blown up: made explode.

brief: short.   **murky**: gloomy; dark.

frantic: crazy; mad.   **glimmering**: reflecting light.

all was over: all was finished.

the gory chief: the chief covered with blood.   **surveyed**: inspected.   **strewed**: scattered.

get used to: be familiar with.

to get you to excuse me: to apologize.

to suit you: in a way that you like.

I am confident: I am sure.

to speak the plain truth: to be honest.   **sort of**: kind of.

is liable to: is exposed to.

yourself: personally.

calls forth: requires.

with comfort: in tranquillity.

this berth: this job.

to wait on: to take care of.

novel: original; new.   **grant**: assure.   **entertaining**: diverting.

after a fashion: in some manner.   **judiciously**: in a good way.

shoots: fires.   **cripples**: injures; mutilates.

stove-pipe: tube of the heating apparatus.

for your gratification: for you.   **stove**: heating apparatus.

drops in: comes here.   **to swap**: exchange.   **freckles *me***: marks me with spots.   **bullet-holes**: holes of projectiles.   **principles**: my organs.   **cowhide**: whip.

tears all my clothes off: tears all my clothes into pieces.   **entire**: complete.   **the easy freedom**: the confidence.   **acquaintance**: someone you know well.   **blackguards**: less important people.

in their war-paint, and proceed to scare the rest of me to death with their tomahawks. Take it altogether, I never had such a spirited time in all my life as I have had to-day. No; I like you, and I like your calm unruffled way of explaining things to the customers, but you see I am not used to it. The Southern heart is too impulsive; Southern hospitality is too lavish with the stranger. The paragraphs which I have written to-day, and into whose cold sentences your masterly hand has infused the fervent spirit of Tennesseean journalism, will wake up another nest of hornets. All that mob of editors will come – and they will come hungry, too, and want somebody for breakfast. I shall have to bid you adieu. I decline to be present at these festivities. I came South for my health, I will go back on the same errand, and suddenly. Tennesseean journalism is too stirring for me." After which we parted with mutual regret, and I took apartments at the hospital.

[1869]

war-paint: agressive attitudes. **proceed**: start. **scare**: fill with fear. **tomahawks**: indian axes. **Take it altogether**: as a whole.
spirited time: animated period.
unruffled: not complicated.
you see: you can understand. **used to**: familiar to.
Southern: of the South.
lavish: profuse; extravagant.
whose: of which. **sentences**: phrases.
masterly: of a master; very capable.
wake up: excite. **hornets**: wasps.
mob: furious crowd. **editors**: persons in charge of a newspaper.

to bid you adieu: to say farewell to you. **decline**: refuse.
on the same errand: on the same purpose; for the same reason.
suddenly: immediately. **stirring**: exciting anxiety.
After which: after saying so. **parted**: separated. **with mutual regret**: both being sorry.

The Story of the Old Ram

Every now and then, in these days, the boys used to tell me I ought to get one Jim Blaine to tell me the stirring story of his grandfather's old ram – but they always added that I must not mention the matter unless Jim was drunk at the time – just comfortably and sociably drunk. They kept this up until my curiosity was on the rack to hear the story. I got to haunting Blaine; but it was of no use, the boys always found fault with his condition; he was often moderately but never satisfactorily drunk. I never watched a man's condition with such absorbing interest, such anxious solicitude; I never so pined to see a man uncompromisingly drunk before. At last, one evening I hurried to his cabin, for I learned that this time his situation was such that even the most fastidious could find no fault with it – he was tranquilly, serenely, symmetrically drunk – not a hiccup to mar his voice, not a cloud upon his brain thick enough to obscure his memory. As I entered, he was sitting upon an empty powder-keg, with a clay pipe in one hand and the other raised to command silence. His face was round, red, and very serious; his throat was bare and his hair tumbled; in general appearance and costume he was a stalwart miner of the period. On the pine table stood a candle, and its dim light revealed "the boys" sitting here and there on bunks, candle-boxes, powder-kegs, etc. They said:

"Sh –! Don't speak – he's going to commence."

I found a seat at once, and Blaine said:

"I don't reckon them times will ever come again. There

Ram: uncastrated adult male sheep.

Every now and then: from time to time. **used to**: had the habit of. **ought to**: should. **one Jim Blaine**: a certain Jim Blaine. **stirring**: exciting. **ram**: uncastrated male sheep.

matter: subject. **was drunk**: was intoxicated with alcohol. **at the time**: in that moment. **just**: simply. **comfortably and sociably**: in a relaxed and friendly way. **kept this up**: continued. **was on the rack**: desired strongly. **haunting**: recurring frequently.

found fault with: found something wrong with.

drunk: intoxicated with alcohol.

absorbing: great.

solicitude: anxiety; concern. **I never so pined**: I never desired so much. **At last**: in the end. **hurried**: went with urgency. **cabin**: poor house. **for**: because. **learned**: was told. **such**: in such condition. **fastidious**: critical. **no fault**: nothing wrong.

drunk: intoxicated with alcohol. **hiccup**: singultus. **mar**: disturb. **brain**: mind. **thick**: great; broad.

entered: went in.

empty: with nothing in it. **powder-keg**: small barrel used for holding gun-powder. **raised**: up.

throat: front part of the neck. **bare**: naked. **tumbled**: not in order. **costume**: way of dressing. **stalwart**: strong; solid.

dim: feeble; weak.

here and there: everywhere. **bunks**: beds fixed along a wall like a shelf. **powder-kegs**: small barrels containing gunpowder.

commence: start; begin.

seat: place where to sit. **at once**: immediately.

reckon: think. **them**: *those*.

never was a more bullier old ram than what he was. Grandfather fetched him from Illinois – got him of a man by the name of Yates – Bill Yates – maybe you might have heard of him; his father was a deacon – Baptist – and he was a rustler, too; a man had to get up ruther early to get the start of old Thankful Yates; it was him that put the Greens up to j'ining teams with my grandfather when he moved west. Seth Green was prob'ly the pick of the flock; he married a Wilkerson – Sarah Wilkerson – good cretur, she was – one of the likeliest heifers that was ever raised in old Stoddard, everybody said that knowed her. She could heft a bar'l of flour as easy as I can flirt a flapjack. And spin? Don't mention it! Independent? Humph! When Sile Hawkins come a-browsing around her, she let him know that for all his tin he couldn't trot in harness along-side of *her*. You see, Sile Hawkins was – no, it warn't Sile Hawkins, after all – it was a galoot by the name of Filkins – I disremember his first name; but he *was* a stump – come into pra'r-meeting drunk, one night, hooraying for Nixon, becuz he thought it was a primary; and old Deacon Ferguson up and scooted him through the window and he lit on old Miss Jefferson's head, poor old filly. She was a good soul – had a glass eye and used to lend it to old Miss Wagner, that hadn't any, to receive company in; it warn't big enough, and when Miss Wagner warn't noticing, it would get twisted around in the socket, and look up, maybe, or out to one side, and every which way, while t'other one was looking as straight ahead as a spy-glass. Grown people didn't mind it, but it 'most always made the children cry, it was so sort of scary. She tried packing it in raw cotton, but it wouldn't work, somehow – the cotton would get loose and stick out and look so kind of awful that the children couldn't stand it no way. She was always dropping it out, and turning up her old deadlight on the

there never was: *there has never been*. **a more bullier**: *bullier*, stronger. **fetched**: took.

by the name of: named; called.

a deacon: an ordained minister, immediately below a priest.

rustler: (U.S.) horse and cattle thief. **ruther**: *rather*.

to get the start of: to deceive.

put the Greens up to: incited the Greens to. **j'ining teams**: *joining teams*; following. **prob'ly**: *probably*. **the pick of the flock**: the best of all. **cretur**: *creature*.

likeliest heifers: most beautiful young cow; *here* girl. **raised**: grown up. **knowed**: *knew*.

heft: raise; lift. **bar'l**: *barrel*. **flirt a flapjack**: turn a pancake in the air. **spin**: weave. **Humph**: exlamation of annoiance.

a-browsing around her: trying to attract her attention.

tin: metal; money. **trot in harness alongside of her**: stay on her side. **warn't**: *wasn't*.

after all: actually. **galoot**: (U.S. slang) vulgar person.

I disremember: *I don't remember*. **a stump**: (slang) a fool.

pra'r-meeting: *prayer-meeting*. **hooraying for:** shouting hurra for. **becuz**: *because*. **primary**: election. **Deacon**: minister.

up: stood up. **scooted**: threw.

lit: landed; fell. **filly**: (slang) maiden.

lend it: give it to use.

warn't: *wasn't*.

twisted: turned. **socket**: hole of the eye. **look**: *looked*.

every which way: everywhere.

t'other: *the other*. **straight ahead**: in a straight line; in front. **spyglass**: a small telescope. **Grown people**: adults. **'most**: *almost*.

so sort of scary: frightening in some way. **packing**: fixing.

would get loose: unfastened. **stick out**: came out. **so kind of awful**: terrible in some way. **couldn't stand it no way**: *could stand it noway*. **dropping it out**: letting it fall out. **deadlight**:*here*

57

company empty, and making them oncomfortable, becuz *she* never could tell when it hopped out, being blind on that side, you see. So somebody would have to hunch her and say, 'Your game eye has fetched loose, Miss Wagner, dear' – and then all of them would have to sit and wait till she jammed it in again – wrong side before, as a general thing, and green as a bird's egg, being a bashful cretur and easy sot back before company. But being wrong side before warn't much difference, anyway, becuz her own eye was sky-blue and the glass one was yaller on the front side, so whichever way she turned it it didn't match nohow. Old Miss Wagner was considerable on the borrow, she was. When she had a quilting, or Dorcas S'iety at her house she gen'ally borrowed Miss Higgins's wooden leg to stump around on; it was considerable shorter than her other pin, but much *she* minded that. She said she couldn't abide crutches when she had company, becuz they'were so slow; said when she had company and things had to be done, she wanted to get up and hump herself. She was as bald as a jug, and so she used to borrow Miss Jacops's wig – Miss Jacops was the coffin-peddler's wife – a ratty old buzzard, he was, that used to go roosting around where people was sick, waiting for 'em; and there that old rip would sit all day, in the shade, on a coffin that he judged would fit the can'idate; and if it was a slow customer and kind of uncertain, he'd fetch his rations and a blanket along and sleep in the coffin nights. He was anchored out that way, in frosty weather, for about three weeks, once, before old Robbins's place, waiting for him; and after that, for as much as two years, Jacops was not on speaking terms with the old man, on account of his disapp'inting him. He got one of his feet froze, and lost money, too, becuz old Robbins took a favorable turn and got well. The next time Robbins got sick, Jacops tried to make up with him, and

eye. **oncomfortable**: *uncomfortable*; uneasy. **becuz**: *because*.

hopped out: fell out. **blind**: unable to see.

you see: you understand. **would have**: had. **to hunch**: to push.

game eye: false eye. **has fetched loose**: has come out.

would have: had.

jammed it in: fixed it in.

as a general thing: generally. **bashful cretur**: timid creature.

easy sot back: felt easily embarassed.

warn't: *wasn't*. **becuz**: *because*.

yaller: *yellow*.

whichever way: in any way.

it didn't match nohow: *it didn't match anyhow*.

quilting: (U.S.) social meeting of women. **Dorcas S'iety**: *Dorcas Society*; charitable society of women. **gen'ally**: *generally*. **borrowed**: took and then gave back. **stump**: move. **considerable**: *considerably*. **pin**: (informal) leg. **minded**: was worried about. **abide**: tolerate. **crutches**: supports for walking. **becuz**: because. **said**: *she said*.

hump herself: walk around.

bald: with no hair. **jug**: a container for liquids. **wig**: artificial hair.

coffin-peddler: seller of coffins (boxes for corpses). **ratty**: (U.S. slang) shabby. **buzzard**: mean person. **roosting around**: staying around. **'em**: *them*. **rip**: dissolute person.

in the shade: repaired from the sun.

would fit: was the right size for. **can'idate**: *candidate*; person who was sick. **he'd fetch his rations**: he took his food.

nights: during the night. **he was anchored**: he didn't move.

frosty: very cold. **once**: one time. **before**: in front of.

place: house.

was not on speaking terms: didn't speak

on account of: because of. **disapp'inting**: *disappointing*; frustrating. **froze**: *frozen*; turned into ice. **becuz**: *because*.

took a favorable turn: got better. **got well**: recovered.

to make up with him: to become friend again with him.

varnished up the same old coffin and fetched it along; but old Robbins was too many for him; he had him in, and 'peared to be powerful weak; he bought the coffin for ten dollars and Jacops was to pay it back and twenty-five more besides if Robbins didn't like the coffin after he'd tried it. And then Robbins died, and at the funeral he bursted off the lid and riz up in his shroud and told the parson to let up on the performances, becuz he could *not* stand such a coffin as that. You see he had been in a trance once before, when he was young, and he took the chances on another, cal'lating that if he made the trip it was money in his pocket, and if he missed fire he couldn't lose a cent. And, by George, he sued Jacops for the rhino and got judgment; and he set up the coffin in his back parlor and said he 'lowed to take his time, now. It was always an aggravation to Jacops, the way that miserable old thing acted. He moved back to Indiany pretty soon – went to Wellsville – Wellsville was the place the Hogadorns was from. Mighty fine family. Old Maryland stock. Old Squire Hogadorn could carry around more mixed licker, and cuss better than 'most any man I ever see. His second wife was the Widder Billings – she that was Becky Martin; her dam was Deacon Dunlap's first wife. Her oldest child, Maria, married a missionary and died in grace – et up by the savages. They et *him*, too, poor feller – biled him. It warn't the custom, so they say, but they explained to friends of his'n that went down there to bring away his things, that they'd tried missionaries every other way and never could get any good out of 'em – and so it annoyed all his relations to find out that that man's life was fooled away just out of a dern'd experiment, so to speak. But mind you, there ain't any-thing ever reely lost; everything that people can't under-stand and don't see the reason of does good if you only hold on and give it a fair shake; Prov'dence don't fire no blank

varnished up: painted with a glossy coating. **fetched**: took.

too many: too intelligent. **had him in**: asked him to get in.

'peared: *appeared*. **powerful**: very.

was to: was supposed to.

more besides: more than that. **tried**: tested.

bursted off the lid: broke suddenly the top of the coffin.

riz up: rose up. **his shroud**: piece of cloth that wrapped him.

to let up on: to stop. **becuz**: *because*. **stand**: tolerate.

You see: you understand. **in a trance**: in a hipnotic state resembling sleep or death. **took the chances on another**: took the opportunity of doing it again. **cal'lating**: *calculating*.

missed fire: was not successful.

by George: by God. **sued**: took to court. **rhino**: (slang) money.

set up: placed. **parlor**: living room.

'lowed: *allowed*. **take his time**: wait. **aggravation**: annoyance.

Indiany: Indiana. **pretty soon**: in a short time.

the Hogadorns: the Hogardorn family. **Mighty**: strong.

stock: race. **Squire**: gentleman.

mixed licker: *mixed liquor*; cheap whiskey. **cuss**: *curse*; imprecate. **'most**: *almost*. **Widder**: *widow*; woman whose husband is dead. **dam**: mother.

et up: *eaten up*. **savages**: primitives; indians.

et: *ate*. **feller**: *fellow*; man. **biled**: *boiled*; cooked in water. **warn't**: *wasn't*. **of his'n**: *of his*.

they'd tried: they had eaten; tasted.

of 'em: *of them*. **annoyed**: upset. **relations**: relatives and friends. **to find out**: to discover. **fooled away**: taken away in a stupid way. **dern'd**: *damned*. **mind you**: note; observe. **ain't**: *isn't*. **reely**: really.

hold on: wait. **shake**: chance; opportunity. **blank**: empty.

ca'tridges, boys. That there missionary's substance, unbeknowns to himself, actu'ly converted every last one of them heathens that took a chance at the barbecue. Nothing ever fetched them but that. Don't tell *me* it was an accident that he was biled. There ain't no such a thing as an accident. When my Uncle Lem was leaning up agin a scaffolding once, sick, or drunk, or suthin, an Irishman with a hod full of bricks fell on him out of the third story and broke the old man's back in two places. People said it was an accident. Much accident there was about that. He didn't know what he was there for, but he was there for a good object. If he hadn't been there the Irishman would have been killed. Nobody can ever make me believe anything different from that. Uncle Lem's dog was there. Why didn't the Irishman fall on the dog? Becuz the dog would 'a' seen him a-coming and stood from under. That's the reason the dog warn't app'inted. A dog can't be depended on to carry out a special prov'dence. Mark my words, it was a put-up thing. Accidents don't happen, boys. Uncle Lem's dog – I wish you could 'a' seen that dog. He was a reg'lar shepherd – or ruther he was part bull and part shepherd – splendid animal; belonged to Parson Hagar before Uncle Lem got him. Parson Hagar belonged to the Western Reserve Hagars; prime family; his mother was a Watson; one of his sisters married a Wheeler; they settled in Morgan County, and he got nipped by the machinery in a carpet factory and went through in less than a quarter of a minute; his widder bought the piece of carpet that had his remains wove in, and people come a hundred mile to 'tend the funeral. There was fourteen yards in the piece. She wouldn't let them roll him up, but planted him just so – full length. The church was middling small where they preached the funeral, and they had to let one end of the coffin stick out of the window. They didn't bury him – they

ca'tridges: *cartridges*; projectiles.

unbeknowns to himself: even if it didn't know it.   **actu'ly**: *actually*; in reality. **heathens**: pagans. **chance**: *here* a piece of food. **fetched**: impressed; convinced. **but**: except.

biled: *boiled*. **ain't no**: *is no*. The *double negative* is very informal.

leaning up: resting. **agin**: *against*.

scaffolding: support used during the erection of a building.

suthin: *something*. **hod**: open wooden box. **story**: floor.

back: spinal column.

Much accident there was about that: you can't talk of an accident.

object: reason.

Becuz: *because*.

would 'a': would have. **a-coming**: *coming*. **stood from under**: would have moved from beneath.   **warn't app'inted**: *wasn't appointed*; was not given that responsability. **carry out**: perform.

Mark my words: pay attention to my words. **put-up**: established.

I wish you could: note the *tense* after *wish*.   **'a'**: *have*.

reg'lar: *regular*; normal. **shepherd**: dog that watches sheep.

bull: bull-dog. **belonged to**: was the property of.

got: had. **belonged to**: was a member of.

prime family: very good family.

settled: established. **nipped**: caught.

went through: went through the machinery.

widder: *widow*; a woman whose husband is dead.

remains: rests. **wove**: interlaced. **come**: *came*.

'tend: *attend*; partecipate to.

planted: buried; put him under the ground.

just so: simply so. **length**: extension.   **middling**: fairly; rather.

end: side.

bury: put him under the ground.

planted one end, and let him stand up, same as a monument. And they nailed a sign on it and put – put on – put on it – sacred to – the m-e-m-o-r-y – of fourteen y-a-r-d-s – of three-ply – car- - -pet – containing all that was – m-o-r-t-a-l – of – of – W-i-l-l-i-a-m – W-h-e –"

Jim Blaine had been growing gradually drowsy and drowsier – his head nodded, once, twice, three times – dropped peacefully upon his breast and he fell tranquilly asleep. The tears were running down the boys' cheeks – they were suffocating with suppressed laughter – and had been from the start, though I had never noticed it. I perceived that I was "sold". I learned then that Jim Blaine's peculiarity was that whenever he reached a certain stage of intoxication, no human power could keep him from setting out, with impressive unction, to tell about a wonderful adventure which he had once had with his grandfather's old ram – and the mention of the ram in the first sentence was as far as any man had ever heard him get, concerning it. He always maundered off, interminably, from one thing to another, till his whisky got the best of him, and he fell asleep. What the thing was that happened to him and his grandfather's old ram is a dark mystery to this day, for nobody has ever yet found out.

[1872]

same as: like.
nailed: fixed with nails.

yard: almost a metre (0,9144). **three-ply**: three layers.

drowsy: sleepy.
nodded: moved up and down.
dropped: fell. **breast**: chest; front part of his body.
tears: drops secreted by lacrimal glands. **cheeks**: faces.

start: beginning.
perceived: understood. **sold**: deceived; cheated.
whenever: every time that. **stage**: level.
keep: refrain.
setting out: starting. **unction**: affection.
he had once had: *he had had once*.
ram: male sheep; mutton. **sentence**: phrase.
concerning: as regarded.
maundered off: talked.
got the best of him: prevailed him.

to this day: till now. **for**: because.
found out: discovered.

A Trial

Capt. Ned Blakely – that name will answer as well as any other fictitious one (for he was still with the living at last accounts, and may not desire to be famous) – sailed ships out of the harbor of San Francisco for many years. He was a stalwart, warm-hearted, eagle-eyed veteran, who had been a sailor nearly fifty years – a sailor from early boyhood. He was a rough, honest creature, full of pluck, and just as full of hardheaded simplicity, too. He hated trifling conventionalities – "business" was the word, with him. He had all a sailor's vindictiveness against the quips and quirks of the law, and steadfastly believed that the first and last aim and object of the law and lawyers was to defeat justice.

He sailed for the Chincha Islands in command of a guano-ship. He had a fine crew, but his negro mate was his pet – on him he had for years lavished his admiration and esteem. It was Capt. Ned's first voyage to the Chinchas, but his fame had gone before him – the fame of being a man who would fight at the dropping of a handkerchief, when imposed upon, and would stand no nonsense. It was a fame well earned. Arrived in the islands, he found that the staple of conversation was the exploits of one Bill Noakes, a bully, the mate of a trading-ship. This man had created a small reign of terror there. At nine o'clock at night, Capt. Ned, all alone, was pacing his deck in the starlight. A form ascended the side, and approached him. Capt. Ned said:

Trial: judicial examination in a civil or criminal court.

Capt.: Captain. **will answer as well as**: will be as good as.
fictitious: not authentic; false. **was still with the living**: was still alive. **at last accounts**: according to the most recent reports.
harbor: repaired port.
stalwart: strong; solid. **eagle-eyed**: very able to see.
sailor: mariner. **nearly**: almost. **from early boyhood**: since when he was a young boy. **rough**: unrefined. **pluck**: courage.
hardheaded: practical; simple. **hated**: didn't like; despised.
trifling: insignificant; frivolous. **conventionalities**: conventional attitudes. **sailor**: mariner. **vindictiveness**: rancour.
quips and quirks: retorts; subterfuges. **steadfastly**: intensively; strongly. **aim**: purpose; scope. **lawyers**: members of the legal profession.
Chincha Islands: islands in the Pacific. **guano**: dried excrements of sea birds. **crew**: men working on a ship. **pet**: favourite.
lavished: given abundantly.
voyage: journey aboard a ship.
fame: reputation.
fight: combat; battle. **dropping**: falling.
imposed upon: forced; disturbed. **stand**: tolerate. **nonsense**: absurdity. **earned**: acquired; merited. **staple**: main subject.
exploits: deeds; enterprises. **one**: a certain.
bully: man who persecuted and intimidated weaker peolple.
mate: officer. **trading-ship**: merchant ship.
pacing: walking on. **deck**: platform of the ship.
ascended: went up; climbed. **approached**: went near.

"Who goes there?"

"I'm Bill Noakes, the best man on the islands."

"What do you want aboard this ship?"

"I've heard of Capt. Ned Blakely, and one of us is a better man than 'tother – I'll know which, before I go ashore."

"You have come to the right shop – I'm your man. I'll learn you to come aboard this ship without an *in*vite."

He seized Noakes, backed him against the mainmast, pounded his face to a pulp, and then threw him overboard. Noakes was not convinced. He returned the next night, got the pulp renewed, and went overboard head first, as before. He was satisfied.

A week after this, while Noakes was carousing with a sailor crowd on shore, at noonday, Capt. Ned's colored mate came along, and Noakes tried to pick a quarrel with him. The negro evaded the trap, and tried to get away. Noakes followed him up; the negro began to run; Noakes fired on him with a revolver and killed him. Half a dozen sea-captains witnessed the whole affair. Noakes retreated to the small after-cabin of his ship, with two other bullies, and gave out that death would be the portion of any man that intruded there. There was no attempt made to follow the villains; there was no disposition to do it, and indeed very little thought of such an enterprise. There were no courts and no officers; there was no government; the islands belonged to Peru, and Peru was far away; she had no official representative on the ground; and neither had any other nation.

However, Capt. Ned was not perplexing his head about such things. They concerned him not. He was boiling with rage and furious for justice. At nine o'clock at night he loaded a double-barreled gun with slugs, fished out a pair of handcuffs, got a ship's lantern, summoned his quartermaster, and went ashore. He said:

'tother: *the other*. **ashore**: onto land.

to the right shop: to the right place. **I'll learn**: *here* I'll teach.

*in*vite: (informal) invitation.

seized: took firmly. **backed him**: pushed him back. **mainmast**: principal support for the sails. **pounded his face to a pulp**: pulverized his face.

got the pulp renewed: had his face pulverized again. **head first**: with his head down.

carousing: drinking.

sailor crowd: a group of mariners. **on shore**: on land. **noonday**: midday. **colored mate**: black first officer. **to pick a quarrel**: to start a fight. **negro**: black man. **evaded**: escaped.

fired on him: shot him. **dozen**: group of twelve.

sea-captains: captains of ships. **witnessed**: were present at.

retreated to: retired into. **after-cabin**: cabin in the rear part of the ship. **gave out**: made known. **portion**: sort; destiny.

intruded: came without an invitation.

villains: bad people. **disposition**: wish; desire. **indeed**: in reality.

courts: courts of justice.

belonged: was the property of. **far away:** very distant.

on the ground: in that place. **neither**: meaning *not also*.

However: anyway. **was not perplexing his head**: was not thinking. **concerned him not**: didn't interest him. **boiling with**: note the preposition *with*. **rage**: fury.

loaded: charged. **double-barreled**: with two charges. **slugs**: projectiles. **handcuffs**: metal rings for securing prisoners.

quartermaster: officer. **ashore**: onto land.

"Do you see that ship there at the dock?"

"Ay-ay, sir."

"It's the *Venus*."

"Ay-ay, sir."

"You – you know *me.*"

"Ay-ay, sir."

"Very well, then. Take the lantern. Carry it just under your chin. I'll walk behind you and rest this gun-barrel on your shoulder, p'inting forward – so. Keep your lantern well up, so's I can see things ahead of you good. I'm going to march in on Noakes – and take him – and jug the other chaps. If you flinch – well, you know *me.*"

"Ay-ay, sir."

In this order they filed aboard softly, arrived at Noakes's den, the quartermaster pushed the door open, and the lantern revealed the three desperadoes sitting on the floor. Capt. Ned said:

"I'm Ned Blakely. I've got you under fire. Don't you move without orders – any of you. You two kneel down in the corner; faces to the wall – now. Bill Noakes, put these handcuffs on; now come up close. Quartermaster, fasten 'em. All right. Don't stir, sir. Quartermaster, put the key in the outside of the door. Now, men, I'm going to lock you two in; and if you try to burst through this door – well, you've heard of *me*. Bill Noakes, fall in ahead, and march. All set. Quartermaster, lock the door."

Noakes spent the night on board Blakeky's ship, a prisoner under strict guard. Early in the morning Capt. Ned called in all the sea-captains in the harbor and invited them, with nautical ceremony, to be present on board his ship at nine o'clock to witness the hanging of Noakes at the yard-arm!

"What! The man has not been tried."

"Of course he hasn't. But didn't he kill the nigger?"

"Certainly he did; but you are not thinking of hanging him

70

dock: pier in a port.
Ay-ay: (informal) yes.

just: exactly.
chin: front part of the face below the lips. **rest**: place.
p'inting: *pointing*. **so**: in this way.
so's: *so as*; so that. **ahead of**: in front of. **good**: well.
march in: walk in. **jug**: put into jail. **chaps**: (informal) men.
flinch: draw back; move.
Ay-ay: yes.
filed: went one behind the other. **softly**: silently.
den: the habitat of an animal. **quartermaster**: officer.

under fire: in the firing line of my gun. **Don't you move**: don't
move. **kneel down**: go down on your knees.

handcuffs: metal rings for securing prisoners. **come up close**:
come near. **'em**: *them*.
the outside: the external part. **lock** : close.
burst: move violently.
fall in ahead: come in front of me. **march**: walk.
All set: everything is ready.
spent: passed.

called in: summoned. **harbor**: repaired port.

to witness: be present at. **yard-arm**: (nautical) part of a mast.
been tried: had a process.
Of course: certainly. **nigger**: black man.
hanging: killing him suspending him by his neck.

without a trial?"

"*Trial*! What do I want to try him for, if he killed the nigger?"

"Oh, Capt. Ned, this will *never* do. Think how it will sound."

"Sound be hanged! Didn't he kill the nigger?"

"Certainly, certainly, Capt. Ned – nobody denies that – but –"

"Then I'm going to *hang* him, that's all. Everybody I've talked to talks just the same way you do. Everybody says he killed the nigger, everybody knows he killed the nigger, and yet every lubber of you wants him *tried* for it. I don't understand such bloody foolishness as that. *Tried!* Mind you, I don't object to trying him if it's got to be done to give satistaction; and I'll be there, and chip in and help, too; but put it off till afternoon – put it off till afternoon, for I'll have my hands middling full till after the burying – "

"Why, what do you mean? Are you going to hang him *anyhow* – and try him afterward?"

"Didn't I *say* I was going to hang him? I never saw such people as you. What's difference? You ask a favor, and then you ain't satisfied when you get it. Before or after's all one – *you* know how the trial will go. He killed the nigger. Say – I must be going. If your mate would like to come to the hanging, fetch him along. I like him."

There was a stir in the camp. The captains came in a body and pleaded with Capt. Ned not to do this rash thing. They promised that they would create a court composed of captains of the best character; they would impanel a jury; they would conduct everything in a way becoming the serious nature of the business in hand, and give the case an impartial hearing and the accused a fair trial. And they said it would be murder, and punishable by the American courts if he persisted and hung the accused on his ship.

trial: legal procedure; process.

try: examine in court of law.

nigger: black man.

do: work.

how it will sound: how it will appear.

Sound: *here* exclamation of anger.

denies that: says that it isn't true.

just the same way: exactly like.

lubber: stupid person. **tried**: examined in a court of law.

bloody: (informal) damned. **foolishness**: stupid things.

Mind you: pay attention. **I don't object to**: I'm not against.

chip in: (informal) contribute.

put it off: posticipate. **for**: because.

middling: fairly; rather. **the burying**: the funeral.

mean: want to say.

try him: examine him in court. **afterward**: after that.

such people as you: people of your kind. **favor**: (U.S.) favour.

ain't: *aren't*.

all one: exactly the same. **trial**: legal procedure.

nigger: black man. **I must be going**: I have to go right now.

fetch him along: take him with us.

stir: movement. **body**: representative.

pleaded: asked insistently. **rash**: impetuous.

impanel: (U.S.) empanel; select.

becoming: apt to; suitable for.

in hand: in question.

hearing: investigation in a court of law. **fair**: honest.

murder: premeditated killing.

courts: tribunals. **persisted**: continued in his idea.

They pleaded hard. Capt. Ned said:

"Gentlemen, I'm not stubborn and I'm not unreasonable. I'm always willing to do just as near right as I can. How long will it take?"

"Probably only a little while."

"And can I take him up the shore and hang him as soon as you are done?"

"If he is proven guilty he shall be hanged without unnecessary delay."

"*If* he's proven guilty. Great Neptune, *ain't* he guilty? This beats my time. Why you all *know* he's guilty."

But at last they satisfied him that they were projecting nothing underhanded. Then he said:

"Well, all right. You go on and try him and I'll go down and overhaul his conscience and prepare him to go – like enough he needs it, and I don't want to send him off without a show for hereafter."

This was another obstacle. They finally convinced him that it was necessary to have the accused in court. Then they said they would send a guard to bring him.

"No, sir, I prefer to fetch him myself – he don't get out of *my* hands. Besides, I've got to go to the ship to get a rope, anyway."

The court assembled with due ceremony, impaneled a jury, and presently Capt. Ned entered, leading the prisoner with one hand and carrying a Bible and a rope in the other. He seated himself by the side of his captive and told the court to "up anchor and make sail". Then he turned a searching eye on the jury, and detected Noakes's friends, the two bullies. He strode over and said to them confidentially:

"You're here to interfere, you see. Now you vote right, do you hear? – or else there'll be a double-barreled inquest here when this trial's off, and your remainders will go

74

pleaded: asked insistently.

stubborn: obstinate.

I'm always willing: I always want. **just as near right as**: as more correctly as. **will it take**: will it last; will it go on.

a little while: a short time.

shore: land near the sea.

you are done: you have finished.

guilty: responsible for the offence.

delay: waste of time.

ain't: *isn't*.

This beats my time: I can't understand this. **Why**: because.

satisfied: convinced. **projecting**: planning.

underhanded: clandestine.

go on: continue. **try him**: examine him in a tribunal.

overhaul: examine carefully.

like enough: no doubt. **send him off**: cause him to depart.

show: chance; opportunity. **hereafter**: the time after his death.

in court: in the tribunal.

would send: *future in the past*.

fetch: take. **myself**: personally. **he don't**: he *doesn't*.

Besides: in addition to that. **rope**: strong cord.

assembled: came together. **due**: appropriate. **impaneled**: (U.S.) empaneled; selected. **presently**: in a short while; soon. **rope**: strong cord.

seated himself: sat. **by the side of**: next to. **captive**: prisoner.

up anchor and make sail: (nautical slang) start. **turned a serching eye on**: looked very carefully at. **detected**: discovered.

bullies: persons who hurt and persecute weak people. **strode**: went. **confidentially**: privately.

right: in the right way.

double-barreled inquest: a trial with the gun.

off: finished. **your remainders**: what remains of you.

home in a couple of baskets."

The caution was not without fruit. The jury was a unit – the verdict, "Guilty".

Capt. Ned sprung to his feet and said:

"Come along – you're my meat *now,* my lad, anyway. Gentlemen, you've done yourselves proud. I invite you all to come and see that I do it all straight. Follow me to the cañon, a mile above here."

The court informed him that a sheriff had been appointed to do the hanging, and –

Capt. Ned's patience was at an end. His wrath was boundless. The subject of a sheriff was judiciously dropped.

When the crowd arrived at the cañon, Capt. Ned climbed a tree and arranged the halter, then came down and noosed his man. He opened his Bible, and laid aside his hat. Selecting a chapter at random, he read it through, in a deep bass voice and with sincere solemnity. Then he said:

"Lad, you are about to go aloft and give an account of yourself; and the lighter a man's manifest is, as far as sin's concerned, the better for him. Make a clean breast, man, and carry a log with you that'll bear inspection. You killed the nigger?"

No reply. A long pause.

The captain read another chapter, pausing, from time to time, to impress the effect. Then he talked an earnest, persuasive sermon to him, and ended by repeating the question:

"Did you kill the nigger?"

No reply – other than a malignant scowl. The captain now read the first and second chapters of Genesis, with deep feeling, paused a moment, closed the book reverently, and said with a perceptible savor of satisfaction:

"There. Four chapters. There's few that would have took

caution: warning. **fruit**: result. **a unit**: unanimous.

Guilty: responsible for the offence.

sprung to his feet: stood up.

Come along: come with me. **my meat**: in my hands. **lad**: man.

you've done yourselves proud: you acted with honour.

all straight: all in the right way.

cañon: canyon.

appointed: nominated.

was at an end: was over. **wrath**: fury.

boundless: without limits.

dropped: put apart.

crowd: great number of people. **climbed**: went up.

arranged the halter: placed the strong cord. **noosed**: put the cord around the neck. **laid**: put down.

at random: not in a prearranged way.

bass: very low.

Lad: young man. **you are about to go aloft:** you will go up in the sky in the immediate future. **manifest**: list.

as far as sin's concerned: as regards sin. **Make a clean breast**: clean your conscience. **log**: book where records of the voyage are made.

reply: answer.

pausing: stopping.

earnest: sincere.

reply: answer. **scowl**: contraction of the brows.

feeling: sentiment. **paused**: stopped.

savor: (U.S.) savour; trace.

There's   few: *there are   few.*

the pains with you that I have."

Then he swung up the condemned, and made the rope fast; stood by and timed him half an hour with his watch, and then delivered the body to the court. A little after, as he stood contemplating the motionless figure, a doubt came into his face; evidently he felt a twinge of conscience – a misgiving – and he said with a sigh:

"Well, p'raps I ought to burnt him, maybe. But I was trying to do for the best."

When the history of this affair reached Californiia (it was in the "early days") it made a deal of talk, but did not diminish the captain's popularity in any degree. It increased it, indeed; California had a population then that "inflicted" justice after a fashion that was simplicity and primitiveness itself, and could therefore admire appreciatively when the same fashion was followed elsewhere.

[1872]

the pains: the trouble.

swung up: hung up. **made the rope fast**: fixed the rope.

stood by: stood near him. **timed**: checked the time.

delivered: gave.

motionless: that didn't move.

twinge: sudden pang.

misgiving: feeling of doubt.

p'raps: *perhaps*; maybe. **I ought to burnt**: I should have burnt.

a deal of: a lot of.

in any degree: at any level.

indeed: actually; in reality.

after a fashion: in a way.

appreciatively: in appreciation.

elsewhere: in a different place.

CONTENTS

Editorial note

In some stories Mark Twain uses a phonetic spelling reproducing the Western slang (ex. *feller*; *reg'lar*; *jest*; *cretur,* etc.) and some expressions which do not follow the standard English grammar (ex. *lots of the boys has seen*; *he give*; *them circumstances,* etc.). In the notes you will always find the standarized expressions written in *italics*.

IMPROVE YOUR ENGLISH
a series directed by Enrica Caimi

Aa. Vv. – **AMERICAN SHORT STORIES**

Gilbert Keith Chesterton – **TWO FATHER BROWN STORIES** (The Blue Cross, The Honour of Israel Gow)

Arthur Conan Doyle – **TWO SHERLOCK HOLMES STORIES** (A Case of Identity, The Adventure of the Sussex Vampire)

Joseph Conrad – **YOUTH**

Rudyard Kipling – **THE LOST LEGION followed by "A Conference of the Powers"**

D. H. Lawrence – **NONE OF THAT**

Jack London – **THE LAW OF LIFE and other stories** (A Piece of Steak, War)

Katherine Mansfield – **THE GARDEN-PARTY and other stories** (The Woman at the Store, The Canary)

Hermann Melville – **COCK-A-DOODLE-DOO! and other stories**

Edgar Allan Poe – **THE PIT AND THE PENDULUM and other stories** (The Tell-Tale Heart, Ms. Found in a Bottle)

Robert Louis Stevenson – **THE BOTTLE IMP**

Mark Twain – **THE CALIFORNIAN'S TALE and other stories** (The Notorious Jumping Frog of Calaveras County, Journalism in Tennessee, The Story of the Old Ram, A Trial)

Oscar Wilde – **THE CANTERVILLE GHOST**